I eagerly recommend
Living With A Limp. The reason is simple. I have
walked with Jerry a long time, I've seen him live with a
limp and I've met few individuals who carry his
measure of wit and wisdom while passing through
life's hardships in such a redemptive, grace-filled way.
The reader will be enriched and encouraged as Jerry
shares out of the legacy of his life. What a gift!

Roger Nix
Believers Church, Pastor
24-7 Prayer USA, Board Chairman

Knowing Jerry Lout is in itself a true privilege and
delight. He has a joy and passion that is infectious. He's
the real deal in that he's learned to cope with, and even
leverage for God's purposes, his running life's race
with a limp.

Jerry's narratives are captivating, heart-warming, and
his style easy to read. I have no doubt that anyone who
reads of his journey will be inspired and encouraged.

Dave Jewitt,
Your One Degree, Founder/Director

My earliest memories trace to the years my father,
Melvin Creason, served as youth minister in a small
town church. Among those under his charge were two
brothers, Tim and Jerry Lout. Jerry's communication
reminds me a lot of my dad. I'm a person who reads
again and again books I really like. 'Living With A

Limp' will remain within easy reach for a long time to come.

Denise Creason Buschman, R.N.

All of us are building our legacy one day at a time. In *Living With a Limp,* Jerry Lout winsomely shares his story of overcoming adversity, of pursuing his calling, as he gleans worthy lessons along the way.

Jim Stovall, Bestselling Author
The Ultimate Gift

The believer sees deficiencies, not as handicaps, but as stepping stones. Problems then become means of increasing our assurance in God. His greatness is our focus.

It was my privilege to serve with Jerry Lout in Kenya. Whatever his limitations, trekking mountains or walking the African bush made no difference to him. Studying the life of the Patriarch Jacob we subscribe to a saying, "Never trust a man who doesn't limp".

Paul Johansson
Chancellor, Elim Bible Institute and College
Founder and Board Chairman, New York School of Urban Ministry

My relationship with Jerry Lout covers nearly 50 years. His personality and lifestyle is a smile. He's lived robustly--knowing setbacks while not succumbing to them. *Living With A Limp*, a collection of stimulating narratives, will encourage and uplift all who've ever been battered in the journey of life. Thank you Jerry for sharing out of your struggles and comforts that we may be comforted as well.

Van G. Gill
International Bible College
Theology Instructor, CAO, retired

Living With A Limp takes us to a simpler time, to Jerry's growing-up years in rural Oklahoma. His encounters with Christ-followers yield up life lessons that find their way to us through his narratives. For decades Jerry has served internationally, faithfully sharing the good news of Jesus Christ.

Those who know the Savior will be stirred to love him more deeply through the reading of these accounts. May God use us to bless others in sharing *His* story, as Jerry has done, even with a limp.

Mickey Keith
Independent Assemblies, President

Living With A Limp

Copyright © 2016 by Jerry Lout

Editing by Jeanette Gardner Littleton
Book Design by Andy Mullins
Photography back cover by Daniel Herold

Printed in the United States of America

First Printing, 2016

ISBN-13: 978-1534678507
ISBN-10: 1534678506

Living With A Limp

Jerry Lout

To ANN,

loving companion, devoted mom and grandmom

charitable servant · treasured friend

CONTENTS

Thanks

Friends Mike and Anita for a memorable hike near their Gallup home.

Author Therese Stenzel, whose enthusiastic editorial work early on put wind beneath my writing wings.

Tulsa's Fellowship of Christian Writers, inspirers all.

Millard Parrish and Terry Ligon. Exceptional proofreading and tech support—the extra mile.

Editor Jeanette Gardner Littleton, skillfully correcting, adjusting, tweaking the manuscript, giving the stream of narratives a much improved flow.

RJ Thesman, author and writing coach for laboring diligently throughout the journey. Capably tutoring, fielding endless questions, adding exceptional insights - always with grace. Alerting me to a host of vital tidbits, principles and practices. All the while praying. That the *Author* of life might gain honor due him through this endeavor.

My faithful blog readers, whose uplifting comments pumped adrenaline to the writing veins during my *blogging-a-book venture*.

My Montana bride, Ann, who has faithfully supported me through this wild, weighty, wonderful venture.

PROLOGUE

Nearing the summit, I slowed my pace. Not used to the thin air of New Mexico's high desert, my lungs labored to keep up.

Across the valley, a freight train snaked along. I closed my eyes considering a young man of another era, a non-paying box car tenant passing this same route many years before. The train's image shrank in the distance. Melancholy drew near.

While celebrating the courage of this man of decades past, I mourned his journey. *So harsh, this travel. Could he not have found another way?*

Orphaned in early childhood—both his parents had died before his seventh birthday—and now, railway lines seemed his only relief.

Home lay miles behind him. The term *hobo* had been directed his way more than once over these past days. The Atchison, Topeka and Santa Fe Railway was his new home–for the present, anyway.

Oklahoma would not see him again, not anytime soon. He was fleeing a dust-plagued land.

2

Croplands craved rainfall. A new term was even coined. The drought was reshaping the plains into a Dust Bowl.

Deprived of parental care, he had a limp of sorts, setbacks in life. Still he pushed forward. Better fortunes lay before him in a new land. If lucky he'd gain work. And food.

I knew this young man. He gave me his name.

4

CHAPTER ONE

The MOTHER ROAD

Clyde Baxter sprinted to the next line of tracks, hoping to avoid the bulls—railroad police—along the way. Increasing his speed beside a moving string of box-cars, he selected one and leapt aboard. A handkerchief partly shielded his face from blowing grime.

A few more days riding the rails and he would reach San Francisco Bay. That was his hope.

His body craved food, but he hungered to find work even more. Still he pushed himself ahead. Better fortunes were coming.

Clyde balanced himself in the box car. He rolled a pebble back and forth beneath his worn shoe. *Well*, he mused, *I have something worth going on for*. He corrected himself. *Someone.*

How would the trim Oklahoma girl make her way safely to California, assuming he could find work? Leaning from the box car, he steadied himself, and looked westward again.

***

Clyde carried something in him that was still being forged, refined through the grit of tough times. Resolve. The quality that's seen in people whose wills are anchored in purpose, in meaning. Where meaning falters, resolve can weaken. But meaning for Clyde, well, it meant something.

Further lessons about worthwhile things lay ahead for him. Some of them would be pleasurable, some would come in the middle of pain.

In later years as a father he shared such lessons with his children. Not verbally so much. Rather, by example, modelling qualities common to men of steady character. Clyde's surname was Lout. I would one day call him Daddy.

***

Taking in the view of San Francisco Bay, Clyde Baxter sampled the faint taste of salt air. Slowly filling his lungs, he considered the untimely passing of his parents. The white plague (tuberculosis) had destroyed *their* lungs. An inner yearning, perhaps the kind only orphans understand, arose within him.

Following their passing, he and his siblings received scant assistance from nearby relatives, themselves fighting scarcity.

The oldest of the surviving children—girls in their teens—grappled with the burden.

"What will happen, Dovie?" Alva worried. "How do we care for the young ones?" Dovie faced her sister with a calm she knew she didn't possess. "We do the best we can, dear."

Clyde pushed his mournful thoughts aside. He boarded a packed bus, jostling with passengers of uncommon accents and language. A wiry man of different features, holding a cardboard box with two live chickens in hand, stepped onto the bus. Clyde studied his manners with vague curiosity. *Could he be what they call an oriental?*

Tales making their way out of California to Oklahoma had brought him and others like him promises of better. Better earnings. Better hopes of keeping fed. Some boasted all-your-dreams-come-true promises. Most did not.

While towns around San Francisco Bay supplied first-time visitors endless attractions, Clyde stayed focused. *It's work I need.*

An observation shared by a seasoned laborer stuck with Clyde. He hoped it proved true.

"Coming to California doesn't mean an easy life, young man. . . but easier? Yes."

Clyde had quit school after tenth grade to grind along in depleted cotton fields for 50 cents a week. No work here could bring so bad a wage as hoeing cotton back home.

Years later, referring to his days of job-hunting around the Bay, Dad remarked without bluster, "I hustled."

Hustle, expressed crisply in Depression-era language meant living by ones wits, making a serious effort to obtain money.

He found work.

The first day at his first job he eyed the shovel handed him, unwittingly comparing its wooden handle's grain pattern to that of a cotton hoe. A foreman indicated a long single row of drainage pipes stretching before them. "Make the trench 20 inches deep."

Clyde's spade cut into the earth. *Well,* he thought, *I am working.*

***

"Clyde, have a look at this." His older brother, Ernest, who had been his one close railway companion westward, passed a flyer his way.

"Hmm, 'Plumber's Helper Wanted'. Thanks."

The new job earned Clyde less pay than ditch digging. At first. But his steady work habits yielded him, in time, a hard-gained promotion.

***

Fishing two silver-headed thumb tacks from a drawer, he secured the modest *certified plumber* certificate to his bedroom wall—opposite his girl's photograph.

A frugal man, his savings grew steadily. He directed his attention more and more to the framed image of his fiancée.

There. She's got her ticket. He looked to a patch of blue overhead, the sky emerging through a lifting fog over the bay. *Don't let anything happen to her*, he mouthed to a deity he hoped was there.

***

Baby, pay good attention—changing buses I mean. I don't want you winding up in Oregon or something. Thelma, be real careful.

Clyde considered their future. They would start life together in a beautiful place where land and waterways met. He smiled at the thought of her last name—Bay.

Life was hopeful. Hardships could wait.

***

Her parents and siblings saw her to the bus station. Her father, nicknamed Toughie by the townspeople, was sober today. Thelma drew comfort from this.

Though he was reasonably civil otherwise, Toughie's drinking binges plagued him and his family. His loud, reckless outbursts sent his wife retreating—not to a neighbor's house but to sanctuaries within her mind. In time the hiding places shrank, leaving her depressed, fragile.

During those days of disorder, the children, hearing from a distance their raucous father stumbling home, found quick excuse to vanish.

"Come right on in here, children," their neighbor Mrs. Walsh called, swinging wide the screen door. The Walsh boys and their ever-present fiddle, guitar, pump organ and vocal cords provided a musical, lighthearted haven for Bay children and others who would drop by.

Steps away now from leaving this behind, Thelma turned to her sensitive, warm mother, Della Bay.

"I love you, Mama. I promise I'll write you letters." In the moment Thelma's tears started to gather, her mind flashing a thousand memories. Releasing hold of her mother, she turned aside.

Clutching her tan cardboard suitcase Thelma stepped aboard the Greyhound Bus. With her free hand she swept a film of dust from an empty seat. Dust was like a crazed intruder. Nothing seemed to deter it.

She settled in. Unknowns lay ahead. *What is it like anyway? This Golden State?*

Still she knew — Clyde was waiting. He had kept his promise. He wired her the money. He would meet her at the other end of the line. *Like anyone*, she considered, *he has faults, but he keeps his word. He sent for me. He wants me*. Her tightened shoulders relaxed. *He'll greet me with his wide smile and hold me close*. Her nervousness eased further,

The bus was on open road now. Thelma lowered her hands, linked her fingers over her midsection and looked out the window. One . . . two . . three — she counted fence posts parading by.

Seated near the front, she couldn't help but gawk at the steering wheel, its size dwarfed that of the old car they'd come to the bus station in. A memory brought a giggle which she stifled with her hand. While he was on a date, her brother Don had been shocked when the car's steering wheel broke free in his hands. Only the clever use of a screw driver to the steering column assured his safe arrival home.

Thirty minutes on the road and the town of Henryetta lay behind. For a time she tried capturing and holding town names of any size, repeating them in order every little while. Okemah. Harrah. Choctaw.

Yukon. Weatherford. The memory game helped through long travel miles. But well before a Texas sign reading *Amarillo* came into view she had wearied of the practice.

An exodus of automobiles and trucks, some barely roadworthy, chugged westward along with the buses. Most bulged with Texans and Oklahomans — Dustbowl escapees. Route 66 — lately called The Mother Road, according to her brother Don — carried them all. Every small town dotting the highway received the caravan and sent them onward.

After more than two days of road travel, her bus rolled the final half-mile toward East Bay's station. *Oh, Clyde*, she breathed, *I can't wait.* The bus drew to a stop, and the door squeaked open. A quick check of her appearance by a window reflection and Thelma was eagerly studying faces of locals receiving their travelers. Her eyes squinted.

Where is Clyde?

Lugging her suitcase, she alighted. She glanced to the big clock and scanned the area until the plaza nearly emptied.

Fingering a scrap of paper with an address scrawled on it, she trudged off.

The suitcase felt heavier.

***

Clyde hurried along hilly streets. He was frantic. Mortified. *How could a guy drift off to sleep like that and miss his girl's arrival?*

Turning another corner he felt his breath catch. Sorrowfully, he took in the scene across the way. Her shoulder sagged. Her face was flushed. The past two days, Clyde had pictured them racing toward each other. Laughing.

Reaching for her suitcase, he hugged her awkwardly. Travel-weary and trembling, Thelma managed a faint smile.

"I'm really sorry, Thelma. . . I'm real sorry."

Entering the apartment he glanced at the couch where, minutes before, he had lain sound asleep. He apologized again.

Clyde was a man of strong conscience. Today it pummeled him.

***

The Oklahoman had long since atoned for his oversleeping bungle. His earnings as a plumbing apprentice helped ready them for a modest but happy welcome of their firstborn. Betty Joann's January arrival came within the first year of Thelma's journey west.

***

Can I hold him, mother?

Nearing her fourth birthday, Betty welcomed her newborn brother to their home.

Thelma let his curly blond hair grow long, prompting passersby to enthuse over the two children, "Oh, what lovely girls."

"Clyde, listen to this, their breathing, It's coming short and strained." He caught the worry in her voice. "This sound, as they take in air. What is it?"

Weeks passed. Betty and Bobby's asthma worsened. The Bay's damp air didn't help. Clyde turned to their mother.

"Thelma, we need to move."

His oldest sibling, Dovie, had settled in Arizona with her family. The Louts left for Phoenix.

Clyde found a place not far from Dovie's and in a reasonable time he got lucky. He found work.

***

"Jack! Jack! Oh, God!" The neighbor screamed wildly, again yelling the appeal. The young man pivoted. His eyes followed her gesture.

The canal!

Irrigation waters had swept Jack's young cousin downstream. The twenty year old ran two and a half blocks before catching up with little Bobby. He pulled the child from the current and onto the canal bank.

***

Bobby Lout's death lunged the family into grief. Thelma anguished over the drowning so intensely her family and friends wondered whether or not she would recover emotional balance. Wailings gave way to sobs, then whimpers—cycles kept alive with renewed sobbing—followed by long silences.

If limping means to falter when walking, Clyde and Thelma and Betty each limped. Every person knows someone who has stumbled—limped—in their inmost selves under grief's weight. Crippling lameness cries for companionship, compassion. For family—natural or otherwise.

Clyde's sister was near.

***

Dovie touched the apron hem to her eyes, dabbed at gathering tears. She released the apron. It fell, again draping her cotton dress. Using a dish towel she wiped the last of the dinner plates. Her eyes were sorrowful. Still they displayed a quiet serenity. Dovie turned from the kitchen sink and tenderly regarded her sister-in-law.

Thelma sat nearly motionless at the table. Soft catches in her breathing testified to sobs reluctant to go away. Her eyes were drawn, weary from the work of crying.

A fan in another room whirred. Dovie lingered, sensing the stillness here as a sacred gift. She moved slowly to the space behind Thelma's chair. Softly she rested her hands on the young mother's shoulders. Dovie's hands were weathered, not from age but from the Oklahoma field labor of earlier times.

Her lips moved silently in devotion, breathing only an occasional whisper. "Father, your peace. Your peace, Lord." The prayer seemed more a statement than petition. It acknowledged nearness.

Thelma sensed the nearness. Tension in her shoulders eased. The nearness was something beyond her sister-in-law's gentle presence. She gave herself to it, and it lingered.

Years later Thelma called up memories. Dovie's closeness, her conversations with heaven—times of the presence. "Dovie quietly came to me. Within moments of her hands touching my shoulders I felt different, actually lighter. It's hard to put words to it. That awful sorrow, its heavy darkness lifted off me. Peace settled over me. It was real, this feeling. A sweetness was in the room, a rich presence.

"Then later, entering the cemetery on that day. I felt I was gliding along. I can't explain. Like floating a little above the ground. The same afterward, following the graveside service."

***

The mourners dispersed. The flower-dotted cemetery reverted to its earlier stillness. Thelma almost whispered her words.

"What is it, Dovie? This presence. It's inside me... in gentle waves. What is this goodness and this... safety I feel?"

Thelma's question hung in the air. The shadow off a Canary Island Palm stretched over the lawn before them.

She hungered for answers. The absence of her earlier grief astonished her. She hoped that the calm would somehow remain. Yet she feared it may take flight. Could she carry on? Her voice was quiet.

"Dovie, will this peace, or the cause of it, be near again if I ..." she corrected herself, "when I need it?"

Questions. She had many and voiced them mostly to Dovie over coming weeks.

Dovie was not a person of complicated notions or grand explanations. She waited. As she sensed a thought forming that brought clarity she pondered it, then offered a response. Otherwise she remained still. Prayerful.

To Dovie, the God she had come to know and love was real. What's more, he was the giver of the Book. She sensed inside, the answers for questions that truly mattered were linked to the precious book. The pages of her own Bible showed uncommon signs of wear. It attested to truth. And to God's presence.

"All I know, Thelma, Jesus is real. It's him. He's the presence." Her words were simple, unsophisticated, assured. She responded this way, it seemed, every time. Always highlighting Jesus.

"How do I get him. . . have him in my life, Dovie? Can I? I don't want to be without the hope. I need Jesus."

Dovie touched Thelma's hand. "Just say that to him, dear. He has promised that when you come near to him, he will come near to you. Give him your questions. Trust him with your whole life. Let him begin to lead. He's listening. He doesn't turn anybody away."

Thelma followed the gentle counsel and grew more peaceful, more assured.

Shortly after, Clyde kneeled, choosing as well to trust himself to God's care. Both of them were ready, keenly sensing their need of God's steadying presence. He could supply it—he who understood better than any the pain of releasing a son to the grave. Neither knew much about doctrine, didn't understand their experience in that way. They did not worry themselves over it. They believed. And trusted.

Clyde and Thelma entered a new kind of life, like being on a new road, one of trust and of following *another*. They were quite confident at times, limping their way along at others. They trusted their wrongs to him, and their hopes. They felt they were getting a father. And a friend. Jesus, their friend.

***

Thelma hadn't been without religious exposure. Years afterward she reflected, "You know, back in Schulter I went for a time to a church, was even asked to teach a children's class. I tried doing that for a while." She paused thoughtfully. "But I never experienced the Lord. During the time after losing Bobby I came to see I could have the Lord really in my life. Really know him."

***

California's Mojave Desert wasn't the ideal dwelling place for a family, but it did supply one perk. Houses didn't cost much. South African immigrants had assigned names to gold mining communities. A two mile drive west of Johannesburg led to Randsburg, where Clyde, Thelma and seven-year-old Betty settled into their new home. Clyde paid $190 for the house. His plumbing skills secured work for him at a nearby military base.

During the agonizing hours after Bobby's drowning, Clyde had privately pledged that he and Thelma would have no more children. His heart began slowly healing as he read through Bible stories. The life and words of Jesus especially drew him in, quieting his soul. He sensed growth on his spiritual path.

Still, something he dreamed after going to bed one night in their small Randsburg home left him astonished.

In the dream he pictured small children he couldn't recall ever seeing before. They were lively, happy at play.

After some moments into the dream a crisp, convicting message, like a theme, overtook his mind: Bringing no further children into the world was not Clyde's decision to make. Not really. His choosing this path closed the door to receiving precious little ones assigned to their family's care.

Receiving? Assigned?

In the days following, Clyde could not shrug off images of laughing, playing children nor the dream's assertion. The matter became a conviction. He yielded.

In due course Thelma delivered their third child. All nine pounds of Timothy Arthur Lout were clearly present. Exclamations erupted at Red Mountain's hospital.

"Now there's a big boy! He's half grown already!"

Timothy was still a baby when the family moved again. Back to the Bay. To Berkeley. My mother later reviewed the setting and its seasons, "When you were born, Jerry, Berkeley was just a quiet little college town."

I came into the world one year and one month and one day after my brother Tim. I skinned up the tip of my nose from regularly rooting face-down against the bed sheets. For this the hospital nurses labeled me "little bull."

How our small-framed mother actually delivered us bruisers, Tim and me, is a marvel. I trumped my brother's birth weight, tipping the scales at a disquieting ten pounds. By all appearances I seemed marked for a robust, healthy life.

But during this period a word was finding its way into conversations across the country: Polio.

CHAPTER TWO

BUBBLING WATER

When the Okies left Oklahoma and moved to California, it raised the I.Q. of both states. -Will Rogers

On a spring night in 1946 my mother had a dream— a vivid one, of our family travelling a long roadway.

"Clyde, I think the Lord could be saying we're to go back to Oklahoma."

His response was almost instant. "Yes, that sounds like a good thing!" They laughed, sensing again, a guiding hand they were growing to recognize. They wrapped up personal matters, gathered belongings, said goodbyes.

Early the morning of our departure, Clyde poured water into the canvas bag designed especially for travelers crossing desert country. "Glad somebody thought up this invention." He looked eastward. "An overheating radiator could cause us a few breakdowns out there. At least I can keep it topped up on those long climbs in the high desert." Securing the water bag to the car's outer grill near its radiator, he slid into the driver's seat. The sun would be rising soon. It would be well into the sky before they turned due east, into the Mojave Desert of California and Arizona. After that, on to the Southern Plains.

My father, Clyde Lout, was a living testament to a rural adage. Dust bowl issues successfully took the boy out of the country and off to California urban centers. Nothing prevailed however at taking the country out of the boy. Oklahoma soil, finally recovered from the drought of the 1930s, had called to him and our mother.

We settled in Okmulgee (oak-muhl-gee)—a Creek Indian name meaning bubbling water.

I was five months old when we entered the land of my family's roots. It would be my land, the place of my roots. We were home.

A crippling disease invaded around my first birthday. We lived on Bryan Street before our move to the countryside. The polio virus disabled my legs and feet before I could hardly try them out. The assault was rapid and, thankfully, short-lived. It contorted my left foot, permanently altering its range of motion. In time my left leg resumed growing but never quite caught up with the other, leaving the left one over an inch shorter. The redesigned foot and shortened leg combined to supply me with an unwanted trademark: a limp.

The intruder wasn't finished.

***

Lively music, clapping hands and shouts of, "Amen!" ascended into the night at Okmulgee's north end. It was summer, 1949. Something called a tent revival meeting had come to town.

In the 1940s and '50s open tents seated 50 to 100 people and served the purposes of transient American preachers. Our visiting preacher, Sister Alva, and her husband oversaw the tent's raising on a vacant lot. A sawdust floor, wooden folding chairs, worn hymnals and a guitar and accordion completed the setting. The tent's older visitors kept hand-held fans in easy reach. Preaching was Bible-centered, the messages vigorously delivered. The singing pulsed with strength.

Clyde and Thelma Lout visited the tent—my sister, brother, and me in tow. The music, preaching and testimonials seemed to usher in the presence. The family never tired of God's nearness in the company of other Jesus followers.

After a few weeks of conducting meetings Sister Alva believed God wanted them to settle in our Oklahoma town. The couple rented a vacant building. They called the new church the *Living Way.*

After the polio experience my left leg was fitted with a knee to shoe brace. When I turned five, the brace came off for good. I was active without it. Lacking the benefit of therapy coaches during that era, my folks simply retired the brace. My limp became more pronounced.

Over time I started thinking, it seems we all may limp, in some way.

***

"Oh boy."

We used the phrase a lot. Depending on what was happening, the two words combined might convey enthusiasm or frustration, or something else. My "oh boy" this time was not enthusiastic.

While Dad brought home enough pay to keep his family housed and fed, our move to an acreage outside town when I was five brought added costs. "We'll need to tighten our belt for a while."

The baby crib I might have long since vacated was still my go-to place at bedtime. Not the usual size for a crib, this one seemed designed with giant toddlers in mind. Our daddy reasoned, "Why spend good money on another twin bed before Jerry's outgrown the one he's in."

Any growth spurt that might be coming was taking its time reaching me and my sleeping quarters. For maybe a year I contrived to outgrow my crib. I recall several times lying on my back on the sheet, stretching every muscle of my body length-wise. The exercise was to make my toe tips reach the crib's footboard while my head kept in touch with the boundary at the opposite end. I longed to whine to my parents, "I'm so crowded in here. . . can I sleep in a boy's bed now?" I was half-worried I might be shaving by the time I outgrew my crib. *Oh, boy.* Relief came as I was entering my seventh year. My full twin bed filled a space opposite my brother's in our shared room. I'd been liberated from the vertical slats too closely resembling prison bars.

***

I fell in love at age five. Her name was Opaline. She was decades my senior, but she was beautiful. Even in braces. Especially in braces.

The Plymouth sedan rolled to a stop in the parking lot of our little house of worship. When the driver's door opened, a metallic glint caught my eye. The driver was exiting her car. The action was a process. She swiveled slowly so both legs, framed in stainless steel braces, dangled to the outside.

What caught my eye next was her face. Angelic? The adjective wasn't yet in my word-store. But yes. A quality beamed from the young woman's face. Almost a glow. Opaline's smile overtook me. That wonder at her smile never left.

Falling in love with Opaline was enchantment, not romance. An unlikely combination of hardware and heart fueled the attraction. How can full-length leg braces and this kind of smile be shared by the same person? Her cream-colored skirt modestly concealed the braces on her limbs. Those braces. That smile. Meeting Opaline spawned for me a long journey of admiration. My gaze lowered to my own limbs—a malformed shoe fashioned by pressure from an equally malformed foot. My mindset shifted. I smiled at the new revelation. I shared a common affliction with an angel!

***

What could a flooded pasture and a paralyzing disease have in common? Perhaps nothing.

We grew fond of the acreage just north of town. Twin pear trees in the pasture, limbs heavy with their treasures most summers, supplied Tim and me with climbing and feasting pleasures. "Don't eat them when they're green!" was our mother's (occasionally-heeded) caution.

My brother Tim and I fought. Not excessively but, as with many close siblings, enough.

By my second year in elementary school I learned more than counting and reciting the alphabet. I added samplings of profanity to my speech skills. Never mind my ignorance of definitions, I picked up the enlarged vocabulary mostly on the school playground.

I practiced cursing on my brother at least once. Angry with Tim over nothing noteworthy I unleashed a stream of language at a far higher volume than was wise. My mother overheard the rants and seized an educational opportunity. I learned about two things. (1) Resourcefulness. The wire-handle end of her fly swatter-turned-switch. (2) Awareness. Of a zero-tolerance policy for profanity in our home. After the experience, if I wasn't fully cured I was clearly more discreet. For a time.

CHAPTER THREE

ROUND TWO

Our sister Betty chose more wisely than her two young siblings did. Such as places to swim.

Tim and I entered the world of swimming near the pear trees. We did not learn to swim in a pond or in the creek running through our farm's pastureland. Rather, we set in motion our first-ever strokes in the pasture itself.

A red-brown waterway called the Deep Fork River snaked through the countryside west of our place. During a late spring season in the mid-1950s, continued rains flooded the Deep Fork. Ongoing downpours overflowed every creek and stream.

Rising waters overtook lowlands, submerging much of our five acres. Once the rain stopped, my brother and I splashed about in the chest-deep mix of water and floating debris. Discovering buoyancy, we propelled our way through tree bark, sticks and limbs, assorted leaves, and hollowed pecan shells—

and here and there, given it was the habitat of farm animals, other matter as well.

My second bout with the polio virus outstripped the first in its cruelty. We never knew if my unsanitary pasture swim factored in the attack.

I was nine years old. My legs simply stopped working.

Behind our house the ground sloped gently downward to a red barn where we boys often played. Beyond this was a pasture. From a window Mother saw my struggle.

I ambled from the barn toward the house. In mid-step my leg gave way. I fell. Lifting myself up I walked a short distance, then went down again. By the third or fourth tumble Mom was hurrying my way. She helped me to the house. Dad responded to her call and we were soon en route to the doctor's office.

Learning of my earlier polio bout the physician assumed this was not likely the same affliction. By now both legs entirely failed to work. I was admitted, my limbs weakened and stiffening, into our local hospital. My condition worsened.

Another physician was called in. He ran tests and soon conveyed his findings.

Poliomyelitis. Round two.

Hillcrest Hospital occupies a spot near downtown Tulsa on historic Route 66. The virus spread rapidly across the country. Hillcrest administrators concisely labeled one of its areas the *polio ward*. The patients—mostly children—were confined to beds positioned at varied elevated angles. The positioning seemed to be dictated by specific treatments needed. Those with strained breathing muscles required a freer flow of air.

Through an open doorway I glimpsed a daunting, one-occupant contraption (a word my dad applied to any curious object). It reminded me at first of a giant tin can lying sideways. Several patients lay each in their own iron lung, their exposed heads resting on a pillow atop a small extended platform. In most cases, I later learned, the iron lungs kept them alive.

We entered a multi-patient room. With my mother's help, a nurse settled me into a waiting bed.

A sudden cramp assaulted my limbs. I grimaced. After a time the pain lessened.

I relaxed a little. And guessed I would be there awhile.

***

"Jerry, here's a gift to keep your feet company."

The nurse on duty placed a 16-inch-long L-shaped board near the foot of my bed. Anchoring it with sandbags, she pressed the soles of my feet against the flat surface of the upright plank, forcing them to a firm, vertical position, toes up. In coming weeks the crude device often brought critical relief. I pressed against it to counteract cramps that could seize my lower calf, thrusting my foot forward and locking it painfully into a ballerina tiptoe angle.

My mom's fly swatter instruction of past times over my poor language met with failure in Hillcrest Hospital's therapy room.

"Hold his hip firm against the table. Steady now. . . Here we go, up with the right leg."

Two people in white—a spindly man and a large-boned woman—stood opposite each other along the therapy bench. I was lying face-up between them. Their job was to apply stretch treatments to paralysis-affected limbs. The therapy helped arrest the stiffening of muscles.

The leg in motion—kept straight as a board by a firm hand my kneecap—rose upward. The stiffer the muscles the greater the strain. And the pain. Up, up until a searing sharpness passed through my leg, prompting me, their child-patient, to bark out a cuss word. Though not loudly.

The therapists shared knowing but not unkind smiles. Neither spoke. Their assignments were clear—these disguised angels—inflicting pain on helpless children. Only later could I appreciate the pain surely felt by them—the therapists bringing such discomfort to children who were unable to grasp the *why* of it.

An Australian nurse, Sister Elizabeth Kenny, had devised an effective treatment to limber up the muscle tissue of paralyzed limbs. Hillcrest nurses wrapped me in confining, steaming hot packs (I can close my eyes today and smell the heavy, moist odor of sweltering chamois-like blankets). Mercifully the blankets held my body in their constricting grip for only short periods.

I never swore about the hot packs. Just the stretch treatments—and only once, as I recall.

***

Remedial pain. Our world is rich with wise sayings. Some of them coach us about preventing pain; others on the actual usefulness of it. In the Lake Victoria region of Africa sages counsel their young, *He who will not be taught by his elders will be taught by the world*.

Our limpings, whether physical or nonphysical, can meet with useful discomfort. In therapy I had barely entered the school of useful pain and had much to learn. I did not do well on some exams. It's true at times today.

My father and mother didn't discipline me perfectly. No parents do. Still, they would have done me no favor by withholding loving, tough correction when needed. Just as failing to supply pain-inducing treatments meant for the patients' best interest would indeed be unkind. An ancient letter reveals a timeless gem, *No discipline seems pleasant at the time, but painful. Later on, however, it produces a harvest of righteousness and peace for those who have been trained by it.* - Hebrews 12

***

My condition worsened. From waistline to feet my limbs went useless. My upper body shriveled, my respiratory muscles weakened. An attending doctor quietly advised my parents, "Your son will not likely walk again."

A stuffed terrier pup, in its own way, consoled me at times. So did one particular nurse—while specialists discussed my case—and the iron lung.

Nurse Deborah discovered me. How, I'm not sure. She wasn't assigned to my care, but I'm glad she appeared.

One night after finishing her shift, Nurse Deborah dropped by. The visit launched a ritual I kept watch for. Her short pop-ins at the door comforted. I probably had a crush on her. The door would edge open, her nursing-capped head tilt into view. We hear the saying, "a smile that could light up a room." Nurse Deborah owned that smile. What made her pop-by-visits priceless was her greeting.

"I'm going now, Jerry. Have a good sleep, I'm praying for you!" And the smile.

Life wasn't dull in the hospital. Not always. I wakened in mid-flight late one night careening to the floor. The next morning I studied their movements as the staff installed bed railings.

The coal-black terrier I called Jack comforted me in ways stuffed animals do. Jack couldn't wish me well or promise prayers like Nurse Deborah. But the furry puppy gave me what she could not—sustained, tangible nearness within institutional walls. Hospital or not, my quarters remained a not-at-home place occupied mostly by strangers. Jack was hardly ever out of reach, often nuzzled at my neck between chin and one ear. It didn't matter which ear.

Mother moved in with her Tulsa niece, Irene and family, at times. From there she jostled on daily bus rides to see me. Her prayer vigils and simply her presence there calmed me.

My daddy's visits, when he could make them, lifted me in a different way. Striding to my bedside he'd align two of his working-man fingers. This formed his strength-test instrument. Extending the fingers before me, he smiled. "OK, squeeze hard, Buddy." By this exercise he checked my gripping power, hoping to see progress from one visit to the next. I looked forward to the drill, each time giving it my best.

But I weakened further. My breathing muscles strained. Doctors consulted about next steps including the iron lung. The frequency of Dad's strength tests trailed off as my fingers gradually became little more than limp tentacles encircling his.

During this time I started hearing visitors repeat a particular collection of words from the Bible. They were from the book of James.

Is anyone among you sick? Let them call the elders of the church to pray over them and anoint them with oil in the name of the Lord.

And the prayer offered in faith will make the sick person well; the Lord will raise them up. If they have sinned, they will be forgiven.

Elders of our church came to my bedside. They and other dear people had already been praying faithfully in their homes, at the church. The caring visitors rested their hands on me.

"Through your dear Son Jesus, Lord, do heal Jerry." For a God whose descriptive name is Father, this kind of childlike praying seemed the natural thing to do.

A change began. Through the next few days my downward spiral slowed, then leveled off. Doctors put the iron lung option on hold as they noted improved, less-labored breathing. Strength increased. Wonderfully my limbs, inactive for weeks, began stirring—as if waking from hibernation. In a short period I advanced from bedridden patient to aspiring wheelchair jockey. Praying friends rejoiced.

***

"You did what?"

I sat in a wheelchair before the man in the white coat. My thin shoulders jumped a little at the doctor's sharp tone. He was not pleased.

"Who told you to stand up?" he went on.

It was Monday morning.

With my improvement, I had been treated to a rare weekend at our Okmulgee home. Sunday afternoon I had sat restfully on a living room sofa while Mom busied herself in the kitchen.

A sudden thought stirred. *Try your legs. Try to stand.*

I gazed at my limbs. They hadn't supported my body for months. *What if?*

Why not?

I wobbled upward, drawing support from the sofa arm. Once fully upright I leaned against the nearest wall. Steadying myself I called out, "Mother. Mother!" She dropped her dish towel and it landed on the floor. Some quick steps from the kitchen and she was with me. She steadied me a little. Then we stood together. Just standing without movement. Upright. My mom and I looked down at my spindly legs—astonished.

Not accustomed to bearing weight, my legs quivered and Mother lowered me again to the sofa. I smiled big. I was eager to tell the nurses—and the doctor. And Monday came.

Being a youngster, I had been scolded over a generous number of misdeeds before. But I was never rebuked for trying to walk. Scolded for using my limbs—by a person whose job it was to restore their use? The thought bewildered me.

***

"Hello... Hello? Help? Help me please?"

About the time I was being promoted from bed confinement to wheelchair jock I fell victim to bathroom phobia.

On the one hand I took pride in the fact I—by myself, with no help—found my way into a small bathroom adjoining the polio ward. What I failed to consider was the lock design of the bathroom door. Once inside, I set the lock without too much effort— click. Reversing the process wasn't as easy. My hand and finger muscles had weakened dramatically from the virus. Struggle as I might, I failed to budge the silver-coated metal latch.

Once my shaky voice alerted a staff, I was reassured. "Hold on. Just hold on in there, son. We're getting you out."

"Is there a long enough ladder?" someone called to another party. I glanced to the single open window several feet up. The anxious voice beyond the door seemed to indicate more adventure than I cared for on this overcast Tuesday. "A ladder?" another person added, "will we actually need to bring him down through the outside window?" Any comfort gained from the earlier assurances dwindled.

"Ah! Here's Joe. Of maintenance. He has a key!" More excited voices joined the gathering just beyond the door. "Don't worry, son. You'll be out of there in a jiffy now." The latch gave a click and the door opened.

The experience, unsettling as it was, failed to lure me back toward bed pan use.

***

Following the puzzling reaction of a doctor over my sudden mobility, I eventually learned that recovery usually requires process. To put weight on my limbs too soon and without proper oversight could hurt—in some cases perhaps ruin—hope for recovery. Inside though, I could not quiet the rush of emotion. I would soon walk. *Walk.*

Within the month I left Hillcrest Hospital walking. Aided by crutches—but walking.

I was glad being at home.

Reflecting on my polio year I trace the nature of my care at Hillcrest Hospital and elsewhere to a special word. Kindness.

Kindness sprang up in numerous ways in the middle of hard things, like homesickness, pain, and at times, anxiety. It just seemed the quality of kindness couldn't be left outside the doors. It came inside the building, into the big polio ward by way of the kind friend, the kind family member, the kind stranger.

A hungry place inside me responded to an often-heard, "Good night, Jerry, I'm remembering you." Kindness.

My feelings drew comfort from a gift-giver's kindness, a fuzzy, if not breathing, Terrier puppy. Countless kind-hearted givers of ten cent coins—the *March of Dimes* drive—lifted the crushing medical costs off blue collar households hit by the virus.

In the end my body itself awakened, I think, to kindnesses of all kinds. Hospital workers, praying friends. And a source much greater.

> *and the lame came to him. . . and he healed*
> *them.*   -Matthew 21

***

I was glad for all the good around. It helped me wrestle the questions.

"Well, your daddy believes it's cancer."

"Cancer? What is cancer?"

Some things didn't make sense. Stroking Blackie's coal-dark head, my fingers moved to a place back of the ears of our gentle-natured dog. The knots felt mean to me—lumpy, mean creatures. Personalizing them seemed easy. Enemies had come after my dog—our dog. I played with Blackie as much as anyone. Little knobby evil monsters, these lumps. Come to take him from us. I didn't want to lose him and couldn't figure why it had to be.

Blackie did not have to wait long.

"Tim," Dad called to my brother. "I need you to bring a shovel."

We laid Blackie to rest in the acreage beyond a row of grapevines.

One evening at the supper table my dad announced discovering a piece of land. "The property is further out. Eighty acres of good land for cattle and crops."

We moved before my 12th birthday. With the move we acquired a new pet, another dog.

Bonnie was a warm-hearted Brittany spaniel mix. She trailed along wherever she found me—barn lot, creek bed, lawn mowing. Bonnie's departure weighed heavier than any loss I knew. Made weightier still by my judgment lapse that day while attempting, strangely enough, to spare her harm.

Mom moved a curtain, her face leaning nearer to peer out the kitchen window. "Jerry, the mailman's come. Go see if he brought us anything. Maybe a letter from Arizona or a post card from my little sister, Lela, in California. Even something from New York."

Most of our relatives lived out West, except mom's youngest brother, Ernie. A Merchant Marine, Ernie's life was at sea. As often as not, his stateside visits were to a New York harbor.

Making my way down the gravel driveway, I failed to see Bonnie trail behind me. Reaching the mailbox neighboring the big Tulsa highway, I brought my finger to the latch of its drop-down lid. Suddenly my side-vision took in a moving image. As I had turned to get the mail Bonnie trotted past me—onto the highway. Pivoting, I shouted, "Bonnie!" Bonnie stopped, turning to my call. In a second, which seemed much longer, she stood—her head tilted—

looking at me. I see her look today. The driver had no time to brake. The car didn't stop. Probably no need.

Bonnie whimpered, lying on her left side off the pavement 50 feet from impact. Her whimpers came irregularly. I knelt and lay my hand on her side. I wasn't ready for the sensation. Instead of a firm, skeletal frame, I felt something like a sack of loose grain under my palm. "Poor Bonnie, poor, poor girl. I'm sorry girl." It was all I could voice. "Poor girl. I'm sorry girl." After some moments I arose. "It'll be OK, girl. The hurting will stop soon." I moved toward the house.

I'll need the shovel again. But first the rifle.

Hard questions come in all sizes, from long to short. A short one kept me awake that night.

Why?

***

I could read well enough—for a seven-year-old. But I felt confused in that earlier childhood time, pondering over another *why?*

I wonder what it's here for, this sign?

What does it mean?

Yes, I know what it says, I thought to myself.

But the meaning. Is there a meaning, really? The questions played over in my mind.

I visited the mystery further, the yet unanswered question. Why?

Standing on tip-toe I stretched my neck upward. I gulped a few swallows of cool water and surveyed again the puzzling notices, marked in bold lettering. The plaques hung above identical, side-by-side water fountains.

Well, I'm sure I am at the right one. I am White, not Colored.

Mother's voice cut short my musings, "Jerry, come along, it's time to get home."

Trailing behind her, I wondered about the plaques. *I don't know any Colored boys. Hmm, no Colored children at all. Indians, sure. I'm Indian myself,* I pondered, glancing to my suntanned forearm.

Daddy says we're part Cherokee. Or Creek.

Outside, I shielded my eyes from the noon sun, craned my neck upward and took in the *five-and-dime* store sign high atop the building's front. I loved working jigsaw puzzles, striving to form a picture matching a cardboard image. The puzzle now in my head wouldn't come together. Pieces seemed missing. The drinking fountain "why?" stayed a mystery.

***

Race was seldom spoken of in our home. A live and let live attitude seemed to flavor much of the region during the 1950s. My dad employed a man from *Colored Town* when his small plumbing business picked up extra work.

A Negro family (as then called) worked our fields for a time. Purchasing the farm had depleted most of our parent's resources, so no tractors moved about the land the first couple of haying seasons. The black family with horse-drawn rake and stationary baler set up shop at the center of our meadow. Joined with them by space though not culture, part of me wanted to get closer to them. I held back—staying just in hearing distance—entertained by their banter.

"Fetch those pitchforks and get busy before I jab you with one!" Laughter broke out often as the multi-generation clan teased and jostled each other in the midst of labor-intensive work under a fierce Oklahoma sun. Straps and harnesses clattered in sync with the snorting of horses. "Gee!" "Haw!"

52

***

Sunday night. Ebony fingers pounced vigorously up and down the row of piano keys. Living Way had again welcomed Mother Grace and her sister. Sharing a single piano bench the two sisters played, sang and exhorted. Devotion to their savior was contagious, propelling those gathered toward thankfulness to God—his big, extravagant love. Years later, East Africa worship events reminded me. People of African roots rarely need coaching on rhythm. The Living Way nights with our special guests attested to it… "Alright, brothers and sisters— tonight we're just wanting to see Jesus.

"Just Jesus. Only Jesus!"

Mother Grace later moved to Tulsa. The next fifty years her name was synonymous with compassionate service. Many among the homeless fondly knew her as Mother.

By that time someone had decided a single water fountain would do. The plaques went away.

CHAPTER FOUR

ANGEL ON CRUTCHES

My dad had a limp of sorts—disadvantages in life. Somehow, in the midst of them, he found strength to look up. Dreams of railway lines, of meaningful work and of starting a family stirred his imagination. *Why not?* dreams moved him to act.

Years afterward, against prevailing wisdom, my *(why not?)* gaze at my pair of inactive limbs rallied my will, raising my focus. I could not generate this attitude on my own and knew it. Hope came from somewhere beyond me. A place above.

Opaline's "looking up" faith marked her journey—in ways different from mine. With equal wonder.

When the glint of sun from her brace caught my eye that summer day, I wondered. *What about this angel-lady person? What about Opaline?*

When still a toddler, Opaline's body gave way to the same disabling illness that later visited my own world. For her, the impact was dramatic, life-altering, long term. Not for months, as in my case, but years.

Polio wrenched mobility from her lower limbs. Rigid braces confined her feet and legs, effectively imprisoning them there. And, like a prisoner whose parole date is postponed, the waiting lengthened. And lengthened more.

The metal hip-to-heel fixtures lent support to her through her first elementary school year. Then another.

"Opaline dear, one of us will be with you in a minute."

With each morning's waking, she engaged the ritual, aided by her mother or older sister, maneuvering each foot into a special shoe. Fitting the cold steel, its leather padding about her dormant limbs. At nightfall young Opaline reversed the process. Detaching the braces, she leaned further forward, manually lifting her legs onto the bed for the night. And lying motionless, Opaline sometimes wondered. *What would normal movement be like? Running, strolling easily with a friend, dancing?*

A child with a ready smile, she carried a peculiar something within—nothing resembling self-pity, none at all. Rather, a feisty resolve—and zest for living. Like a confident distance runner, Opaline entered the marathon of life. Nothing, it seemed, could sideline her. The theme song of her journey might have been, "Life's an adventure. Bring it on!"

She grew up, completed high school, then college. Friends in our church community regarded her warmly with smiles spreading at her approach. Neither the crutches nor the braces mattered to anyone. She was Sister Opaline.

Sister Opaline, Sunday school teacher.

Sister Opaline, vacation Bible school director.

Sister Opaline, high school teacher (her "handicap-fitted" car carrying her to waiting students in the community of *Dewar* a distance away).

Sister Opaline, Christmas play director. . .

Delightful Opaline.

What's more, she owned her personal imperfections.

Opaline looked to encourage others—especially the younger others. Parading either gossip or whining into Sister Opaline's presence proved simply futile. Her knack for winsomely shifting subjects was magic. She mined for the best in people. Seeing in them their plusses, not minuses—oblivious, it seemed, to short-comings. Her naiveté was flagrant.

Wherever she seated herself, Opaline's crutches lay at the floor or leaned at a wall nearby. Her underarm muscles suffered from bearing her body weight through the years. Still, her face easily sprang into a smile. The smile seemed visually fragrant like a rose coaxing a passerby to inhale.

Our church minister and the people who worshipped together strove to trust the Bible and its message of God's big love—and of his ready power to heal, even do miracles. Meanwhile, at night I fretted.

***

Will tonight be that night, the one when I breathe my last?

Jesus, keep me breathing. Alright, Jesus?

For a while I carried the fear. Especially at night – before drifting to sleep. Not always, but for a long enough period during my childhood, sleep times were worry times. Traumatic? No. Anxious? Yes.

Strangely enough, words of an odd little prayer I had set to memory, fanned the apprehension. I didn't generally think so much of death or of dying—just every night—offering that petition,

Now I lay me down to sleep, I pray the Lord my soul to keep.

If I should die before I wake, I pray the Lord my soul to take.

The four phrases speak the word die only once, but the little word filled up my bedroom.

If I should die—die—die.

Die filled my closet, and the floor space under my bed. The word lingered at the breezy window curtain behind which I suspected the Grim Reaper waited.

At any rate, every night I made sure the poem-prayer moved (most typically in a whisper) through my lips before sleep took over. My insurance until daylight.

Thankfully, by act of will, my mind could lock in on other phrases in the prayer. These settled me. Somewhat. *Keep* my soul. Or (should my life indeed end), *Take* my soul.

Apart from the polio seasons, my childhood passed in general tranquility. Except for times when a curious prayer seemed to hijack my calm.

***

As a nine-year-old, with the aid of crutches, I had walked out a hospital doorway. After months of grave illness. After a doctor predicted I would not walk again. After prayer. By all accounts, through simple trust in a loving healer my astonishing recovery came about through a kind community persistently appealing to him in prayer. Was this a faith healing? To the church family it surely was. God had touched me, and radically so.

And yet there was the matter of Sister Opaline. Would she soon have her miracle?

At a particular church service one Sunday evening I watched keenly, hopefully.

The gangly movements of Angel-lady moved over to the center aisle. Then toward the front.

She was slightly over five feet tall. Her smartly-groomed auburn hair fell an inch or two above her shoulders. Beneath the shoulders, I saw the ever-present crutches. They bore her along, steadying the balance of a lady hardly a hundred pounds heavy.

Opaline positioned herself in the prayer line.

The visiting minister had taken up his Bible and preached on growing in our faith for healing and other important needs. He invited all those hoping for God's healing touch to come forward.

Several people with ailments entered the center aisle. They started toward the front, a mini-pilgrimage for the hopeful. The regulars of the church watched as their friend Opaline joined with others. Her friends were moved. The lady's Christ-like example constantly inspired. Most uplifting was her simple, certain love for Jesus. With her shoulders elevated slightly from the rigid crutches supporting them, Opaline inched forward in the line.

She had lingered there at other times, trusting a miracle of healing might one day come. She could linger again now. She held strongly to a certain knowing. A healing grace from her Lord *would* come. Still, she conceded that the *when* was not hers to decide. She rested in the trustworthiness of a now-

and-not-yet principle often at play in God's wise workings: His ways and timing—perfect and good.

For Opaline there was no question as to whether Jesus healed, nor whether she or her condition mattered to him. She knew that she mattered. He confirmed his love and presence often. In many ways. She felt it, knew it inside. And she responded by loving in return. Loving him. Loving people. Now, here in the healing line as in other settings, she was just ready; open for whatever he may have for her. It was Opaline's way.

The church family looked on, and prayed. They were hopeful, almost straining to believe. Indeed if a miracle could be willed into being (faith aside) her friends would have already seen to it.

With a kind smile the minister greeted her. Sharing scripture—one, perhaps two verses—then prayer.

Nothing. Moments of hopeful lingering. Nothing.

The minister's words came graciously. "Continue in trust, sister. And be at peace." A slow swivel. Opaline retraced the path to her seat. She drew her Bible to its familiar place on her lap. Clasping her hands on it she lifted her heart in petition for those up front, receiving prayer.

Years lumbered by. Indeed the years themselves seemed to even limp at times. Variations of the healing-line scene replayed occasionally. A preaching message, the invitation for healing, Opaline at times joining the others. Crutches, braces, her distinct angular limp navigating the center aisle. Returning in moments—her hardware companions carrying forward their duties into another day, and week, and year.

If Opaline was disheartened, evidence escaped notice. No sorrowing looks of disappointment; no clues of sadness.

Maybe her mindset became, *Perhaps next time.* Maybe, though one likely knew. Regardless. If her spirit did need rallying—it surely rallied.

Opaline was a deep well. Interior graces like contentment and peace and endurance—in the middle of whatever suffering—deepened her, flavored her. Prayer and solitude and worship. These cultivated the graces. She chose—aware of her frailties both inner and outer—a kind of lifestyle she felt most natural to Jesus. Her inner deepening was traced to her frequent times with him. Worshipping Jesus was central to Opaline. No time for wearying whys or for self-pity snivellings. 'Life's an adventure. Bring it on!'

Decembers came and went. Christmas plays never floundered. Summer vacation Bible school was clock-work on.

Opaline's Sunday school children bounced and giggled when she entered their brightly decorated room. They showed off coloring work and clay figures; it didn't matter the quality. Only the meaning mattered. What message from God was each child here to catch today? That view separated the treasured from the trite. Her high school students moaned on any rare day she might be absent. They loved the engaging, gifted instructor. And her smile. Always the smile.

Opaline lived. Limping toward her miracle.

Long ago at a wedding festival where Jesus was a guest, an exuberant voice called out, "You have saved the best till now." - John 2

For Opaline he did the same.

***

"We'll carry you. Like we did in the winter times, Miss Opaline. Please stay. Keep teaching."

Her students treasured this auburn-haired teacher of geometry, shorthand and English.

At times during the winter, icy patches lined a critical high school passageway. It was a short outdoor walk linking classroom areas to school restrooms. With unassuming gallantry senior boys of Opaline's class carefully lifted and carried her to the Ladies Room door. Her crutches, they feared, didn't stabilize her enough to get her safely there and back. Teenaged nobles-in-disguise, they wouldn't chance her risking a fall.

But now it was time. Opaline accepted that she could no longer teach. Her failing health dictated it.

Traces of gray marked her temples and lines of aging graced her forehead. It wasn't her age, though, but a cancer diagnosis that provoked the decision. Opaline loved teaching. She always had. "We'll carry you up and down the stairs to your classes. Anywhere you need, if you'll stay, Miss Opaline."

We lame people—any of us—need carrying at times, it seems. A childhood friend recently called up a scene from my polio journey. She watched on a Sunday as my father carried me into our place of worship. He settled me onto a pillow, cushioning my bony frame. Opaline, as a child, was carried to school and back on a gentle horse. Her siblings accompanied her, walking alongside.

Facing her condition now, Opaline's faith underscored an important truth. Mortality means dependency. All mortals need carrying now and then. She knew she needed carrying in this life and would need carrying into the next. The thought didn't alarm her. It reassured her. The attractive squint in her eyes, familiar movements at outer edges of her mouth, testified still to joy. Her Lord carried her now. He would carry her going forward. Regardless.

Opaline passed her church duties to others she had long mentored. She came less and less for the worship gatherings. At last she was moved to Tulsa's St. Francis Hospital.

I was outside the country when notified of Opaline's death. The message from Oklahoma was simple, "Sister Opaline is now home." Shortly afterward, however, I learned her home going was far from ordinary.

My minister friend, Melvin, sat not far from the hospital bed. He observed Opaline's responses to what she seemed to visibly witness of the other side, before passing on. Pastor Melvin spoke of the wonder of her descriptions.

Nearing the end, Opaline rallied. Her eyes opened wide—then wider yet, as though waking up in another setting. It seemed, indeed, she was.

Her face beamed a radiant Opaline-smile. She was in another place, taking in vivid sounds and scenes.

"Oh! The colors, the beautiful colors. . . like none I've ever seen, like none I could imagine! Oh! And the flowers, such beautiful gardens. . . Beautiful, so beautiful!"

Her voice trailed. Her eyes closed. Moments later with revived energy and her freshly wakened smile, Opaline resumed the adventure—witness to marvels of her own home-going. *Sounds,* this time, captured her attention.

"What glorious music! The singing and the music are so beautiful. I can't imagine. How lovely and beautiful. Oh! Lovely, glorious!" Again her voice faded. Her eyes closed.

Not long after there was quiet. She was gone.

I have thought a lot about our lives, Sister Opaline's and mine. The polio battle. Our similar and differing journeys. I've wondered of prayer. Of God's will. Wondered about a curious mystery—of the miraculous. I've grown confident of something. That, in the experiences of both, the miraculous was in play. Throughout. The supernatural of God intertwining our worlds, ensuring his purposes.

At age nine—aided by crutches to be soon laid aside—I limped from a hospital. Amazingly I soon ran. Freely and in the strength of renewed limbs. All the evidence of the experience virtually shouted, *supernatural*—the work of a wonderful, powerful God.

And then, the miracle of Sister Opaline.

Courage, stamina, her giving-switch ever at the *on* position. They're marks not of a merely good person—tough, resilient, resolute. Years of rich, contagious smiles in the face of adversity, pain, and surely some disappointment. Opaline's life radiated the supernatural. Truths of grace and of joy and of love sounded out most clearly from the very platform of her limpings.

I occasionally draw aside in my mind, entertaining a visual.

The scene is the glorious garden she had taken in during those final hours in a hospital room. Opaline has now just entered the garden and taken the sunny path leading further in. She's clothed in garments of colors beautifully suited to her glorious appearance.

Looking down, Opaline is quickly overtaken with joy at those things she discovers are not present. Leg braces, forever gone. Tedious wooden crutches, not to be found. Up ahead at an open place along the trail of color and fragrance stands a young man of regal bearing. He is clearly a king, majestic in every sense. His face is clearly visible, even at this distance, radiating delight, warmth, peace. Her breath catches.

Before Opaline can complete her low, worshipping bow, his hand extends to her. She hears laughing in his voice. "Come, my dear one. Come!"

Rich orchestra sounds have overtaken the garden.

She races forward like the new creation she has become. They dance.

I eagerly expect and hope that I will in no way be ashamed, but will have sufficient courage so that now as always Christ will be exalted in my body, whether by life or by death.   - Philippians 1

CHAPTER FIVE

POWERS THAT BE

"You'll sleep out in this guest building tonight, Jerry. With Lawrence."

"OK," I acknowledged my uncle's matter-of-fact words.

I didn't know Lawrence. Not really. He wasn't a family member—near or distant—and I wasn't even sure why he was there.

Lawrence was old enough to shave. I was a young boy whose voice still resembled a girl's. The one thing worse than sounding like a girl was when a client called my plumber dad on our home phone. My high-pitched answer often prompted the mortifying, "Hello, Mrs. Lout? Is Mr. Lout in?"

The night in the room with Lawrence was the worse night I had ever known.

I did not know why Lawrence did the things he did to me. What would I say the next morning? Or ever? Who would I tell? Clearly no one. No one. That night, I sensed, for no understandable reason, must never enter my mind. Bewilderment, confusion, shame. Emotions swirled. This had never happened before. I never knew that such a thing could happen. For a child of that era abuse carried no name.

One form of lameness is crippled thinking. From that day and other days that followed, I came to think in unhealthy ways about myself. And of God . . . perhaps especially of God. A vulnerable child, taken beyond their powers to dark places, can go lame. Sometime for years to come. I hobbled internally. Something—I couldn't say what—was wrong.

Just plain wrong.

***

Stargazing.

An outdoor summer night during my early childhood I tilted my head back to glimpse the sky. I took in a sharp breath at the array of stars, far more than I'd ever seen, twinkling back at me. Slipping to the ground I soon lay on my back. A breeze stirred. My eyes wouldn't move away from thousands of glittering lights above me, horizon to horizon.

So many. So, so many.

The term vast hadn't entered my collection of words as I took in the wonder of the stars. A bull frog sounded from our west pond. I was taken by wonder—and I wondered.

How can all these stars be. . . how can they be so many? I pondered their formings, how they might have been made, put there all across the skies. *What kind of maker makes all this, this world and sky and stars—and me?*

I went on with questionings, my mind undistracted by a growing orchestra of crickets and locusts.

Is the one who made them the one the shepherd boy David wrote songs about? "When I consider the heavens, the works of your fingers, the sun and stars you have made . . ."

From that night stargazing became a favorite summer pastime for me. On the practical side, I learned that trying to watch them long periods required lying flat on my back. Chigger bites and the miserable itchings they fostered hindered me at times, but never enough to cure the hypnotic spell. Lying down, even at the risk of the pests, paid off—

and spared me a sure neck crick I'd have gained earlier by long gawkings upward with tilted head. A relative who was knowledgeable about things like planets and galaxies stretched his arm and finger straight overhead one night.

"See up there, where I'm pointing. Keep your eye on that brighter-looking star. Because it's not one." I stared and stared at the penlight inching westward, wowed by this new satellite trivia.

How's it even possible? How can people—plain old people—do that kind of thing . . . send those things way out there. To space?

The fact of God never seemed unlikely to me. How could there not be God? How? Of course. Somebody—somebody really, really, great, really big, and really, really, smart—is back of all this. *Wow. Wow!*

Littleness followed after wonder. *How little this place is, this earth. Sure doesn't seem small to me, not usually, anyway. But it is. Really tiny.*

Placing my fingers before my eyes in the half-light, studying their form, considering a softball glove enclosing them, I gawked. And wondered more. *And me? "Little" isn't even the word.* Refocusing the Milky Way, I whispered, *I'm so little. So little.* Again I recalled David, the Shepherd-king. His song,

> *When I consider your heavens, what is mankind that you are mindful of them, human beings that you care for them?* - Psalm 8

***

I gawked at the time piece lying face-down and open before me. Its shallow metal cover had been removed by my father and he was giving me a ring-side seat to surely one of the world's seven great wonders. The silver-plated pocket watch, its cover scratchy and faded from much use in many settings, steadily ticked off the seconds. It was a working man's watch and its flat, circular face had yellowed with age.

For some reason just looking at that instrument and its moving parts—lying there doing the kind of things time pieces do—stirred feelings somewhere inside me. I hadn't yet been schooled in the term *wonder* nor in its meaning. But recalling the moment I first witnessed the miracle of a pocket watch in action, words like wonder and awe seem to lack force to capture my feelings of that day. The feeling seemed similar yet different to when I had my first sight of a calf being born. And even the moments afterward as she struggled her way up on wobbly shiny-wet legs and drew near her attentive mother. Whose rough tongue, in turn, cleared away some filmy matter clinging to the newborn's coat.

It seemed I couldn't grow tired of peering into the spellbinding world of spinnings and clickings and tickings of my daddy's mighty pocket watch. As with my star-gazing, I seemed nearly hypnotized through those moments. Not in the way a magician at our County Fair claimed to do with his swinging timekeeper on a chain. But by those little interconnecting pieces in motion, clicking off thousands and thousands of seconds every day.

Such powers, those of planets and stars and pocket watches.

I had known power—of a much different kind—an unkind power where an older, stronger boy could do wrong things just because he could. These other powers though, the kinds that sprinkle points of light like a million lightning bugs high above our world—I felt again they pointed me to the best kind of power ever. A *maker* who makes good things, bringing beauty and good to everything. I felt pleased about his kind of power, a power busy at giving, at blessing, not of taking, not for hurting.

I put a question to myself about that watch. *How did someone get all that stuff—those copper-like teethy things and the shinier flat round pieces and the winder-upper thing. How did they get it all together and put it in there and make it work?*

Seeds of an astonishing notion I had thought on a little got watered further in my imagination.

Made things are made.

People make stuff. Watches and airplanes and bobby pins. And, what's more, we all get our own start—we people—somewhere. Sure. God. He's the good power. The big and kind maker. Even when we mess some of the things up that he made.

Like ourselves.

***

Click-thump—click-thump—click-thump.

My shoes mocked me. I never thought a set of footwear could mock. Or embarrass. Or harass. But in the world of a self-conscious adolescent they could. And did, it seemed, with an impish tinge of spite.

In the worst place by far, this school hallway.

Polio had sent me to the hospital after I started fourth grade. Released months later I resumed my schoolboy life.

I'll never forget the first day back in school, my introspective self in great form. *Boy oh boy, me, the only person in the whole school, bumbling down the hallway, held up by these clumsy crutches.* When my legs became strong enough that I could part with the crutches, I felt like skipping. On the inside, I did.

I was probably the most self-conscious kid in the history of Wilson Elementary—and afterwards of Preston Junior High. The discarded crutches became memories, but not my limp. My limp remained as part of me—a reminder of my lameness. I didn't really know the word *stigma.* I just embraced its notion. What I couldn't shake was that aggravating click-thump mantra.

The culprit was the arch of my left foot— rather the absence of an arch.

My first polio bout left me with the keepsake—a left foot with a diving-board-flat arch, and non-functioning tendons. I had nothing to give the foot lift. So the left shoe didn't know how to step—only to clunk or thump to the floor. My right foot, by contrast, arched especially high, like a startled cat. The contradicting sounds my shoes offered while crossing any surface were striking. My efforts to tread softly failed to ease the disgrace. To my introverted ears the klutzy movements bellowed like a braying mule.

It strikes me as amusing sometimes now—my shoes and me. Our perpetual, private shouting match of those years.

Click-thump!, click-thump! "shouting" upward from the hallway floor at me. Myself, in turn, scowling downward, offering a silent retort, *Just shut up!*

Graduation day ended my years of limping self-consciously along high school corridors. The fact didn't comfort me as much as it might have. I slowly realized something.

I had wasted a lot of time looking down.

Today I try to remind myself (when my lazy left foot catches and sends me into a clumsy stumble). Obsessing over my deficiencies serves a purpose. But not a noble one. It shifts attention from the more-than-sufficient benevolent Creator, to my very inadequate self-sufficiency. It leads me to choose anxiety over peace. A poor tradeoff every time.

I began finding my most paralyzing afflictions aren't physical ones, regardless how confining. Indeed, a lot of my limping—worry-centered limping, for instance—issues from paying attention to concerns that are really of no concern at all.

***

A year after my second polio bout I tasted my first cross-cultural experience. What a taste it was.

Fellow fifth-grader Billy lived half the distance that I did from Wilson Grade School. Evenings after school, we would walk to his place, wave bye to each other and I would move on. This Friday was different. A half block before reaching his home we caught the most glorious aroma. The harshness of summer heat had passed. September's milder air had come.

"They're Gypsies," Billy simply remarked as we neared the empty corner lot where a family, arrayed in head scarves and colorful clothing had set up two small tents, their makeshift housing. I had never known a Gypsy.

"Come boys! Come on here. We share our goat!" Threads of smoke arose and lingered above a crude barbeque spit. Over a small flame hung a roasting animal that Billy and I now surmised to be a kid goat. Our lips, mouths and inner throats moistened.

A smiling man with wrinkled features moved naturally toward us. "Here, take this one!" The man held a long fork which, in turn, held a fresh cut of juicy meat. Billy's eyes widened with delight when the savory treat touched his tongue.

"Ah!" the man laughed, "you like!"

Taking the sample offered me, I thanked the gentleman. Relishing its taste—I've found nothing to really compare until now—I moved on, waving goodbye to Billy. Feeling a curious closeness toward this family, after only the few seconds we shared, I wondered. What if everybody treated strangers the way these folks treated Billy and me.

A warm feeling rose inside me. A smile easily followed.

***

"Mother, Mother! Tim's getting clobbered!"

Sprinting through the front door I blurted the report. My mom's face conveyed both alarm and puzzlement.

Tim? Fighting?

My brother survived the fracas. But the image itself seemed crazy. A samurai wrestler in a delicate ballet twirl would be more probable. Today's incident involved a thuggish brute who happened to spot a random kid—my brother—and pouncing.

Actually, Tim did fight. Not in this way. He fought throughout most his lifetime, and with valor.

Tim's actual fighting was about goodness. Indeed, Tim fought to be a good person. To those near him, though, his struggle toward goodness appeared to be hardly a struggle at all. So often it seemed he breathed goodness. For me, his kid brother who more typically breathed mischief, this was disconcerting.

Once our dad suspected us of cigarette smoking and approached me about it.

"Do you boys sometimes smoke?"

"Mm, well, I think Tim might." Mischief.

But I idolized my big brother. We were little when I overheard mother say to a friend, "Tim doesn't eat tomatoes. He also dislikes coconut and, oh yes, pineapple." This was intel enough for me. If Tim shunned these things there was good reason for it. Mom could mark them off her grocery list.

I did acquire a taste for all three foods later in life after I finally sampled them.

Tim went to war against impoliteness, rudeness, and discourtesy. Years after our childhood days I heard him say to his California Bible class, "A practice in our home is to reserve the phrase 'Shut up' for only addressing the dog."

I admired him. I envied him. And I was ticked with him. Why did my brother need to be so stinking pleasant? And compliant?

Detecting goodness in him was fairly easy. Not stuffiness, though. He wasn't Goody Two-Shoes but was loads of fun. With a year and a month and a day separating our ages we did a lot together.

We climbed things.

We climbed trees: pear trees, pecan trees, willow trees. I watched Tim fall from one.

He fractured a wrist, and his reconfigured forearm held me hypnotized the whole way to the hospital. Though clearly hurting, he handled the ordeal well. In the 1950s a bone fracture was a big deal. To set his arm the nurse put him under with ether-soaked cotton. For Tim, it set in motion a bout of serious vomiting. He was miserable and didn't make a fuss. No whining. Not a complaint really. I was impressed. Wow.

In our teen years Dad introduced useful outlets for our climbing zeal. He referred us to the steering wheel of a farm tractor. We climbed aboard. And many times thereafter.

Hay season found Tim steering the big red Farmall. He towed a mowing piece to the meadows. Once cut, the grass lay under the July sun to cure. My squatty orange Allis Chalmers required bailing wire to keep the shift controls in second gear. A multipronged hay rake followed behind the Allis. Once I raked the long grass into windrows, Dad wrapped up the process. He drew the grassy aroma into his lungs. Then he guided his equipment to finish the baling operation for that meadow. It was winter feed for his small cattle herd.

Tim and I kept climbing. Livestock chutes at the rodeo grounds across from our farm. Perched above the bull pens, we adjusted our straw hats and rested our chins on the heels of our open hands. Like the ranch men did at the animal auctions. What fun— up here with my big brother. Adjusting our position, we surveyed the grown-up wranglers practicing their calf roping.

We didn't tire of climbing. The two of us climbed onto the back of Old Bill. Riding horseback meant free entrance to our annual rodeo events— even riding double qualified.

The most thrilling climb was to the top of Greenwood Lake's High Platform. The platform reigned. Well above the water surface, it overlooked the diving boards further down. Greenwood — beloved pond-turned-swimming hole at the edge of town. And the platform. Stationed behind my brother I looked down and shivered. Tim was standard-bearer. If Tim was gutsy enough to fling himself out over the waters from way up there, well.

My brother Tim and my sister, Betty—each influenced me toward good. They conveyed wisdom, even unconsciously at times. Each brought significant insights my way at some crucial times. One of the harshest—and most helpful—statements I took in as a kid came at me through Tim's clenched teeth.

During an especially obnoxious stage of my teenage years Tim shocked me to sanity. Or at least moved me to consider it. Annoyed again by my asinine antics he abruptly turned my way. He had had it with me this time. His voice leveled.

"You know, Jerry, you're a punk. That's what you are. Nothing but a punk!"

His words seared. Like a hay hook going in. Tim had rebuked me with good cause at other times. But this is the time I remember. Following the correction I assessed, as well as I might, the words, *nothing but a punk.* I resolved to work hard at changing. Over time I recognized punk-behavior more when I saw it. Until that rebuke, I hadn't seen it—really seen it—in myself. Years later I reminded him of the strong medicine he dispensed that day. Tim didn't remember it.

We laughed.

***

The young woman beamed. Stepping to the podium she almost sang the announcement.

"Ladies, listen up. You are all invited to Friday night's baby shower for, Jerry Lout!"

My brother's wife Geri—pronounced Jerry—would soon give birth to their first child, Todd Benjamin Lout. Excited female voices rippled through the chapel while the elbow of a buddy seated next to me found its target. My ribcage flinched, "I hadn't heard the news", he grinned, "and you're not even showing!"

After high school and a stint of vocational training Tim had begun work as a draftsman in southwestern Oklahoma. He met Geri there. She became the love of his life.

The Lout brothers moved, each with our brides, within the year of our respective weddings.

These had occurred only two weeks apart of one another. Each of us felt God drawing us to service, neither of us sure what that actually meant. Our first stint at training was in this south Texas College.

Though my brother modeled gentleness and goodness, Tim saw early on that his heart wasn't at home in God—a form of limping common to all at some point. He needed rescuing, needed what the Bible calls training in righteousness.

Clinging to news of a rescuing God who, at great personal cost, opened the way for him to be well on the inside, he trusted himself over to Jesus Christ.

A draftsman concerns himself often with two things—construction and its detail. Tim's draftsman-to-minister shift made sense. Wherever he served as pastor, as counselor or friend, he brought his heart. Each person counted, with his or her unique concerns (detail). He also helped grow people, aiding their progress in spiritual formation (construction). Leaning into a close experience with Christ he entered broken lives of others patiently. In faith. With compassion. Among those was Karena, who attests

with tender frankness, "He saved my life." Karena—
Tim's future daughter-in-law.

Once when he was little Tim swallowed a
roofing nail. Almost. An image of this is branded in my
memory.

Six-year-old Timmy suspended, head
downward, his ankles secure in our daddy's grasp.
Shake. Shake. Third shake. The nail bounced twice on
the living room floor. Breathing resumed—for Tim
and the rest of us.

Memories from childhood can rekindle pain or
prompt feelings of remorse. But some memories
thankfully evoke humor, warmth, and smiles:

Seeing young Tim recklessly bounce along,
approximately straddling a runaway Shetland pony.

Witnessing his just-opened, warm Dr. Pepper
explode upward—redecorating our kitchen ceiling.
Following this with his self-conscious chuckle (Tim
never outgrew his chuckle).

His hilarious mimics of Inspector Clouseau . . .

Teaching himself, then me, guitar. And
singing—lots of singing—carrying through all his
lifetime.

The abdomen pain started in his seventh decade near a birthday. Tests followed. Procedures were scheduled, including pancreas surgery and chemotherapy. The regimen blurred the calendar. Praying people prayed. Cards and calls came.

The decline advanced. His wife summoned hospice care. Geri primarily attended him, at times with the aid of my RN wife and me.

The end drew near, his promotion looked close at hand, and the family had already begun feeling his loss.

One early afternoon I brought a stool. Sitting at his bedside I took his hand. He seldom spoke now. But with eyes still closed, his lips formed the half-sentence, and he sounded the words clearly,

"There is a friend who sticks closer. . ." Just that. A partial sentence.

"Yes, Tim."

I completed the Bible verse from Proverbs he began. It would be the final exchange between us.

"Yes . . . closer than a brother, Tim. And he is here for you, and he's here for me."

He had asked if I would officiate a service should it be needed.

"I would be honored. Still, though, we keep looking to the Father."

I rose early Saturday, July 10, 2010. Heaven had received my brother home four days earlier. This morning we would worship God and celebrate Tim's life.

I made my way to the coffee maker in the kitchen. Reentering my sleeping quarters I reviewed some notes. The room was still. I was reflective.

Consulting the ancient scripture for solace or wisdom never disappointed, I thought. Opening my One Year Bible I turned to this day's reading. July 10.

My breath caught slightly. Familiar words— especially of a recent day—tenderly seized me. Of all the Scripture verses—tailored by a random editor of a random Bible-reading program. I double-checked the reference and the date. Yes, this is for today:

There is a friend who sticks closer than a brother. - Proverbs 18.24

I savored its special message a moment longer. For myself. For all who would take it in. And looked upward.

Thank you, Father. Thank you for Jesus. Thank you for my brother. Tim.

CHAPTER SIX

CONSIDERED CLASSIFIED

"I'd be OK if you'd get your shoe out of my mouth."

The Studebaker pickup lay on its right side—the two uppermost tires slowly spinning.

The poor headlights had failed to alert the inexperienced driver—me—in time. The sharp bend in the gravel curve had taken me by surprise—the road was named Sharp Road for a reason. I braked hard, swinging the steering wheel left. In the time it could take to say 'mishap' I capsized my dad's hay truck. It lay there immobile, like a roped calf waiting for the cowboy to bind its legs.

My heart and head churned. I slowly exhaled. His saucy tone aside, my friend's response brought relief. David was OK. I wriggled up and out the driver-side window. David followed.

Without comment we scanned the shadowed form. Crouching beside the vehicle we took hold, unthinking. An adrenaline-rush may alone account for what followed. We put ourselves into a three-second lifting endeavor. The tires bounced once. Done. Trembling a little, I wondered about any telltale damage along her faded blue side. But the pickup sat erect under the night sky, and that was the main thing. I turned the ignition. It fired and we drove away, our latest experience. And our secret.

The next evening at supper I scrambled for a response to dad's offhand question. I'd been dreading such a moment. He directed the question casually to my brother, Tim, and me.

"Would you boys have an idea about what happened to the sun-visor on the Studebaker?" The visor was metallic, fitted to the outside, above the windshield. Since the previous night on Sharp Road the sun-visor featured an obvious new dip along the passenger side.

Tim, able to honestly plea ignorance, looked puzzled.

Following a pause I attempted a detached tone I hoped would convince.

"Maybe a bale dropped onto it when we were loading hay from the barn loft."

The answer seemed to satisfy dad. He would learn of his overturned truck when I broached the topic years later—when the risk of forfeiting my driving license was well past.

Deception: the act of making someone believe something that is not true; the act of deceiving someone.

Character flaws display themselves in different ways. Generally—thanks to values my parents and other responsible adults drove home—I was a fairly honest kid growing up. But my deception limp surfaced periodically, no question.

To my regret, when I deceived, I deceived on purpose. That said, I didn't usually scheme much in advance. Not always. Things would simply happen, and it was then I schemed. Typically to avoid consequences over some foolishness.

Richard Nixon's after-the-fact scheming made the term 'cover-up' famous. But I appreciated the concept well before Watergate days. My dad's sun visor question provoked for me a scheming diversion on the spot—*maybe a bale dropped. . .* A shotgun blast gave rise to a cover-up that required less scheming.

"Let's go chase down a rabbit."

Our mother cooked the best fried rabbit dinner—supper, as we called it—her green beans, mashed potatoes and gravy perfecting the meal.

Tim gave the summons. Bearing the shotgun with care, he led the way. Passing through knee-level pastureland, we scanned the long Bermuda grass before us. Soon a cotton tail leapt from the grass. Taking speedy hops before Tim could aim and fire, she bounded into a sanctuary, a pile of discarded lumber and tree branches.

We devised a plan. I slipped around to the other side of the tall heap of rubbish to flush out our prey. I was out of Tim's view. Our excitement over a great rabbit dinner may have clouded our judgment.

Balancing on my better foot I attacked a tree branch with the other and shouted, "Out of here Bunny. Out!" The rabbit darted into Tim's view.

I heard the gun blast, felt a burning pain above my left knee, and heard my own scream, all in one alarming moment. I seized the injured leg with both hands and went to my knees. The pain lessened and when no blood appeared my panic eased.

My poor brother came into view, bounding over a log. His face was colorless. Tim gawked at my hands, still in their tourniquet pose. I unfastened my blue jeans and inspected the area above my knee.

Two bluish-red welts.

A few buckshot from the blast had ricocheted—only two of them finding me. They resembled BBs and lacked the speed to break the skin.

The rabbit escaped.

Tim and I suspended our hunting for a later date—taking care to consider the matter of gun safety. And we schemed that afternoon, in a simple collusion of silence. Nothing concerning this particular hunt—nothing—would be shared with anyone. No one.

After a few years when we had left home, we volunteered the account to dad. Meanwhile we killed, dressed, and—trusting to our mother's kitchen graces—ate our share of rabbit and squirrel.

I began warming to a kind of behavior code. Confessing is best done earlier than later. Regardless, confessing—though not fun—is a good thing, period.

When I was fifteen I stole and drank an orange soda from another school's canteen. Three or four of us guys slipped into an empty room off a deserted hallway. Empty, except for the un-chilled soft drinks stacked in crates by the pop machine. We each took a bottle and downed its lukewarm contents. Yuk.

No one spotted us.

The infraction haunted me. After several days of misery I found a pen and paper.

"I am writing to apologize for taking an orange soda without paying from your school's canteen recently. I am sorry. Enclosed is payment for the drink."

The stamped envelope bearing no return address left with our postman that morning carrying a ten cent coin and my unsigned note. Sodas cost a dime in 1962, and I lacked the courage to identify myself.

Confessing is best done when the offender has a name, I knew. That said, confessing was still good.

My conscience was quieted and my dishonesty limp was lessened. I felt I walked a little straighter on the inside. It was a good feeling.

Still, character training was yet in season and I suspected any notion of completing the course right away wasn't too likely.

Confess your sins to each other and pray for each other so that you may be healed. The prayer of a righteous person is powerful and effective.

James 5

***

My father and mother lost their first son to drowning. Given such trauma I am thankful for the courage they showed later when their two boys following reached swimming age.

Tim and I loved water. If it were roomy enough to swim in we weren't picky about the spot. Mom and dad freed us to that pleasure.

Farm ponds and rivers—summertime could find our friends and us reveling in them. The deep blue of rain-filled rock quarries called us. Their depths were bracing, invigorating. At the bottom of one quarry rested a long-abandoned dump truck.

Years before, the truck had somehow rolled from the quarry ridge. It rested submerged there now—still upright. What fun to inhale deeply, dive, navigate the cab interior. Taking turns we mock-drove the old truck until straining lungs sent us aloft to gulp in new oxygen. Then back again, chasing one another through one open window and out the other.

And there was *Greenwood*. "Ouch!" Our buddy Chet laughed as he jumped aside. "What pool around has perch swimming up to nibble at your legs?"

Our favorite swimming hole by far was this pond-turned-commercial pool. A few years earlier, a visionary gentleman at the edge of town had added diving boards, changing rooms and a snack canteen to his large pond. A brilliant revenue source, his family's Greenwood Lake opened for business. It seemed that all the kids in Okmulgee County frolicked in Greenwood at some point before reaching their middle teens.

A lifeguard pulled me from the Lake unconscious early one season. My headfirst dive might have fractured my neck. Thankfully not. The accident sprang from a miscalculation.

Swimming season was freshly opened. The winter months and springtime had brought little rainfall and the shoreline revealed it. Not factoring this, I assumed the lake owners had extended the shoreline—providing a new sliver of beach area.

I trotted onto a small jetty leading to diving areas further out. Stopping short of the diving boards I turned and faced the water, ready to dive.

In previous summers the water here had been several feet deep. Being a pond, the cloudy waters kept me from seeing bottom, judging its depth. There was no new beach. Greenwood was simply low. I dived into water that was inches deep.

I woke up face down on the grass, the lifeguard at my shoulder. An onlooker remarked, "That kid was lucky, looks like he'll make it." Minutes later I swam out to join my brother and our cousin— Aunt Dovie's son, Paul, visiting from Phoenix.

Some ventures seem to usher curious wonders before God's inattentive children. At times they may link us to something—someone—beyond ourselves. Pedaling my bike away from Greenwood that afternoon, I massaged the back of my neck with my free hand. I wondered that maybe a big invisible dad made sure a lifeguard was around and paying attention. *Maybe God sent an extra angel along.. Both of them—lifeguard and angel—there to rescue a real dingbat today.*

***

Among southern dwellers, some of the most sought-after goodies are those growing on trees.

"There's a way to earn yourselves a little spending money, boys." We turned to our dad's voice. His counsel was simple and—like himself—sensible. Tim's dark eyebrows lifted in an, *I'm interested*, way.

Next afternoon we entered Dunhams, a pecan-merchant at the west end of town, bearing merchandise. "Bring your gunny sack over this way, boys. Let's see now," pondered the man weighing our mini-crop. "At thirty cents a pound. . . ."

Rewarded for our labors, our spirits buoyed, we all but strutted from the store. Pedaling the bicycle home—with me balanced on the handle bar—my brother chimed, "Some of Mother's pecan pie with a glass of milk sounds good, huh." My mouth moistened.

***

Horace's old sedan churned dust as it entered the meadow. Dad's hay-baling equipment broke down occasionally, and he called on the hired fix-it man to lend aid. His car was generally white—everywhere but the wide, dark streaks of tobacco stains adorning the left side—from driver window to tail light. These and many other details frame the haying enterprise—all pursuing one aim: feeding our small cattle herd through the winter months.

To my knowledge, nothing of the sheep family ever grazed our property. Perhaps the nearest to it was my purchase of a goat years later. I fattened it up on the old property in advance of my son and his bride's wedding. Their rehearsal dinner featured nyama choma (Swahili for "roasted meat").

The terms sheep and shepherd found their way into our thoughts, however—And often into even our prayers. My family's church culture introduced intriguing words and images like this. Stories to do with sheep and their shepherds drew our family to fondly consider attributes of God. We learned of his nature and of his disposition to us his children. In view of these things, our dad reflected on the blessings that came his way, his good fortune.

A principled man, Clyde Baxter labored for the well-being of his family. The dream of securing employment drove him to ride the freight cars westward. Clyde married Thelma only after establishing himself as a steady wage earner with a stable future. Life carried uncertainties as in every generation. He understood this and stayed focused.

Linking his work ethic to his modest ten grades of schooling, Clyde excelled in the plumbing craft, eventually launching his own small business, City Plumbing, of Okmulgee.

His love for rural life stirred. *What if?*

So dad moved his shop to our 80-acre place a mile from town.

"OK boys, get up. Time for Sunday school." Throughout the busy years Dad did the best he knew to give us a moral and spiritual footing.

He sensed that his abilities to labor, to plan and to provide rose from a wiser influence. He knew he was not a self-made man. But he entered into and drew from a source greater than his human ingenuity could supply.

The grown-up orphan knew from his experiences in the faith, he was fathered. And shepherded.

Our dad was reserved. His prayers were private. In my growing-up years it was sounds of my mother's intercessions that drifted from their room. Mother petitioned the shepherd. When we gathered at mealtime, it was always mother blessing the food.

My child mind's eye resonated with images of a shepherd. Jesus was shepherd. He was more. Jesus was good shepherd —giving all for his sheep. From my earliest years, exploits of a giant-slaying, lion-crippling, shepherd boy fired my imagination. And each October Sister Opaline selected Christmas Play characters. I was thrilled at arriving for practice one or two seasons cast as a shepherd. A long crook staff in hand I saw myself as a kind but commanding presence. Protector of the defenseless.

Shepherds watching their sheep by night. Wow!

Through vivid Bible scenes I witnessed Jesus stepping beyond a gathering of well-sheltered lambs and ewes. In the dark, the good shepherd went looking. It was for me he came searching. I was the strayed sheep. I saw myself lying helpless in a distant ravine, wolves prowling nearby.

One Sunday morning in Bible story time the teacher invited me to welcome the good shepherd into my life. "He laid down his life for you, Jerry—a helpless sheep, gone astray—a lamb he loves so much. Your heart is like a door. He stands just beyond, outside knocking." The wording was straight out of the Bible, near the end. Guided into a simple prayer I eagerly believed, opening my heart's door.

Jesus came. His Spirit entered my life in his mysterious way. And I knew.

Jesus really is my shepherd, my good shepherd.

Today I know him in a wider range of wonderful titles – Savior. Friend. Teacher. Brother. Comforter. King. Father.

As a limping, sometimes straying sheep, I cherish him still as I first came to know him.

The Lord is my shepherd; I lack nothing.

\- Psalm 23

CHAPTER SEVEN

MORE

A gravel parking lot where two streets met hemmed in our little white church. Inside I scooted my trousered bottom cautiously along an unpolished church bench —taking care to dodge the occasional splinter. I gave in at times to a curious temptation— running my finger-tips along the bench's underside. A braille-like search yielded my prize: a random trail of chewing gum deposits—discarded and hardened. I don't recall ever sampling more than perhaps one. Oddly enough, their presence supplied me with a sense of comfort—contentment derived from revisiting a familiar setting. Like being home.

Living Way church was home in certain ways. Clyde and Thelma Lout set the worship-attendance tradition in motion from the start: Sunday morning and Sunday evening, Tuesday, and Friday nights. Four services every week. Increased to a fifth—the youth meeting—when my brother and I entered our teens.

The Living Way.

Where with fellow preschoolers I first sang, "Jesus loves the little children of the world."

Where a bearded prophet parted a sea, an inn-keeper denied a couple lodging, an unflustered Messiah calmed a wild storm. I witnessed it all through the magic of flannel graph.

Where ponderous sermons from Leviticus on "types and shadows" lulled me to sleep

Where people prayed fervently over me against a life-threatening virus.

Where the mystery of presence descended on eleven-year-olds one summer morning.

***

"Isn't he just wonderful, boys and girls?"

The portly gentleman exuded joy. With no pretention. Clearly Brother Madison loved Jesus.

Warmly commanding by nature, Brother Madison was an established businessman in town. A lay minister, he served in a spiritual renewal movement among Christian professionals. He delighted in aiding others toward a vital relationship with his Lord. We children—seated in the vacation Bible school assembly that morning—knew Brother Madison. We liked him. And trusted him.

"How many of you youngsters would like more of him. More of Jesus in your life?"

Hands went up speedily. Of course. Who wouldn't wish for more of the good shepherd's presence?

We were ten to twelve year-olds. It was summertime and our third day in vacation Bible school. Brother Madison's words conveyed invitation, and our expectancy-barometers rose. What's coming? It seemed something special could be ahead. What does having more of Jesus mean? Some of us wondered.

Addison acknowledged our raised hands.

"That's wonderful." His smile was large and warm.

He summoned us to a pair of benches near the front of the chapel. He directed the girls to one; the boys to the other. Brother Madison passively jingled coins in a pocket, letting us settle in. We knelt along one side of the benches.

"Now boys and girls, we are all up here because we simply want more of Jesus. We open the way by speaking to him. Speaking our love to Jesus," he continued.

"Begin now to think of Jesus. What he is like? How good he is. How caring. And thanking him. Let's speak our thanks and our love to him.

"Yes. He is meeting us here. Just now. In this place. We welcome him. He is good. And he loves us. He comes among us now. Bringing more. More. Speak to him. Let him speak to you in your heart. Let him love you. He's here."

We offered our voices. Each spoke softly, sincerely. To Jesus.

Without trying, we began sensing him. We were aware. Even as young children. Then, hardly a moment passed and something happened I will never forget. Would never wish to.

Every child—perhaps fifteen or sixteen—was suddenly awash in delight. Rich, bubbling up delight. It overtook us in a moment's time.

And tenderness. Our pre-adolescent eyes poured tears. Self-consciousness went out the window. Words rolled from us—some intelligible, some otherwise. We didn't care. We had yielded over for more of Jesus. And we knew he had come—in wave on wave of tenderness, love, delight.

We cried over and over our love of him. Then, as if on cue, we sought one another out. We rushed — bawling, laughing—to embrace other kids. Anyone in reach. Every boy found another boy or two to hug and to laugh and to cry on and with. Among the girls the same was true. Mucus and laughter mingled in the pleasure of affection not one of us had known. Ever.

The phenomenon carried forward a good while. No child took interest in snack time. Cookies and Kool-Aid could never match this.

We were loved. And we loved. We couldn't love one another too much. We couldn't cry thank you too much. Love and thanksgiving poured over us like water over Okmulgee Lake's spillway in a wet spring season. We knew this was Jesus moving among us, filling us. I hoped this could just go on and on.

After a time, quiet came—the most serene sort. Purity bathed us. What words capture this? The purest of pure soaked the atmosphere. Today I would employ a companion word: holiness. We little non-theologians were immersed in holiness.

Brother Madison spoke a simple encouragement of letting Jesus fill and refill us as we would afterward go our ways.

I relish this richer-than-rich memory—personal, sacred marvel that it was.

Six decades have passed. While I have, by God's kindness, savored many cherished times in his presence, I suspect I may never taste a sweeter, richer flavor. When, at age eleven, one summer morning my friends, and I said, "Yes". To more.

You make known to me the path of life;
you will fill me with joy in your presence.

-Psalm 16

CHAPTER EIGHT

SPARED

Oblivious to the drop-off lying just ahead, I drove the tractor directly toward it. Squeezing the jostling steering wheel, I stayed moving at a good clip—clueless to the danger ahead. The Farmall I steered was a large machine—even to a grown man. And I felt very grown today, this, my first tractor solo drive. I was thirteen.

Satisfied with his tutoring session of minutes before, Dad had directed me to slow the tractor to a crawl. Stepping off the vehicle's drawbar, he followed by foot.

I reached forward. I'll draw this lever toward me across those little metal teeth—pick up some speed.

The engine belched. I felt the tractor buck slightly and gather speed—stretching the distance between my father and me. Tall grass still obscured the drop-off straight ahead. The tractor was going to the ditch. Me aboard. Oblivious.

Suddenly a breeze caught my dad's whistles and shouts. They fought their way over the competing clamor of the tractor I sat upon.

Puzzled, I shifted position and looked back. I wonder what Dad wants?

He was a blur of action—like a physical trainer and Olympic sprinter morphed. Arms swinging wildly, he ran with everything. All the while he shouted, "Stop. Stop!" Clearly this was urgent.

My right shoe found the brake pedal, and I shoved it vigorously. Dust swirled near the big tires. I killed the noisy engine, and a deep quiet took over. Only then did I take in the actual scene before me. My eyes widened. The Farmall stopped feet from the bank's edge—just short of me tumbling headlong into the creek bed. In slow motion a thought began forming in my brain. A chill passed through me,

I think my dad just saved my life.

***

We had three tractors in our farm tractor collection. Ever frugal, Dad bought one only after it gathered a lot of miles—plowing fields, working hay meadows, wheat harvests.

We kept a squatty Allis Chalmers and two of the sizable Farmall Hs.

One of our Farmalls, perhaps the one spared a ditch plunge, featured in another close call. A firearm also factored in.

Following a Sunday dinner a young fellow visiting our home joined me to try spotting a squirrel. We dismounted the tractor near a wooded area.

"Let's try the trees along this creek bed."

Twenty-two rifle in hand, we scouted nesting spots with no success. The day was warm and we shuffled back to the tractor. I settled into the driver's seat. "Step on up," I said, indicating the draw bar back of me. "Take a seat up on the big tire there."

My new acquaintance sat facing me, his feet resting on the broad axle housing, the rifle lying across his lap. After a quarter hour of killing time, I started the engine.

Unthinking, I shifted to forward gear and released the clutch.

Memory retention is heightened when crises occur. Vivid details branded themselves to my mind. A little reflection can cause a post-panic shudder, even after the years have passed.

Thrown forward to the ground, the kid was on his back. His body—in the path of the advancing tire—faced upward toward me, in a near fetal posture. The sole of his shoe was inches from the hovering tire tread. He held the rifle crosswise, extending it as if to ward off the thousand pounds of tire and axle rolling directly his way. *What if* questions take me to the spot even today. *What if my reflexes had been too slow? What if the brake hadn't engaged?*

Once again—providentially it seemed—a boot found a brake pedal and thrust it downward. Once again, stillness. And pondering.

When spared the horror of toppling a tractor and myself over an embankment I reflected with some emotion, *My dad just saved my life.*

In the later near-miss, I considered the other dad. In the language of an earlier time the Bible speaks of God as Abba—a tender, endearing term. Father.

Again I mused.

Abba saved my friend's life being taken. Saved me from taking it.

I looked to the blue beyond the high tree branches.

Thank you.

For this reason I kneel before the Father, from whom every family in heaven and on earth derives its name.   - Ephesians 3

***

Dad busily plowed a fifteen-acre piece of land. Lifting his straw hat, he motioned me his way. I patted my horse's mane.

Famous cowboys of TV westerns labeled their horses captivating names: Trigger, Silver, Scout. Their riders, Roy Rogers, the Lone Ranger, Tonto, mounted their steeds and sped after the bad guys. When Dad brought our 15-year-old gelding to the farm, we carried on with the horse's original name.

"Giddap, Bill."

Responding to my boot heels at his ribs and a right tug to his rein, he turned and galloped toward the tractor.

Throttling the noisy engine down, my father assigned me an errand, "I need a short length of rope. One's up at the garage."

Minutes after leaving my dad, I lay writhing, half-delirious where my horse had fallen in our barnyard lot. I cried out. My leg felt it was on fire.

Bill had gathered himself from the fall and stood wide-eyed nearby. He was perhaps reviewing in some horse-like way the experience of moments ago. A momentary quiet settled over me, my 14-year-old mind barely in touch with the surroundings.

In a way that seemed strangely comforting, my nose took in the sharp, raw smell of cow manure. Another burning pain shot through the leg. My renewed shouts broke the calm. In moments a pair of rescuing arms hauled me up from the barn-lot earth.

My brother-in-law, a decade my senior, was at our farm. He had run toward my screams. Inspecting me, ruling out broken bones, he gathered me up.

"Open the screen. I've got your brother. He's hurt."

Soon my grubby frame, smelling of horse sweat and trampled hay, lay on the green couch in our living room. I had survived. I never learned whether the rope I was to fetch made it to my dad.

My horse would carry me to the pastures again. I was comforted by this.

***

They decided and that was that. They deprived him any say: no decision-making leverage, no voicing an opinion. Not that it would have mattered. They were the farmers. Bill was the horse.

To him it probably seemed unfair. Bill didn't sign up to entertain adolescent boys, have their spurs gouge his ribs at will, yank the bridle this way and that until the bit bruised his mouth. Who turns teenage boys loose to traumatize a stallion—not to mention a 15-year-old gelding?

Such injustice may have prompted the biting assault to my side one fall day.

Neither my brother Tim nor I —nor our Dad for that matter—was schooled in proper horse care. Still, we weren't mean to Bill. Not on purpose.

Added to other abuses, the reckless cinching of a saddle strap can be especially annoying, evidently, to a horse.

He was a tall animal and at first stood passively as I brought the saddle upward along his left side. Landing it atop the protective wool blanket I reached beneath and across Bill's mid-section for the strap. Bringing it my way I threaded it through the cinch ring. I then undertook the most demanding task in preparing for an afternoon ride, apart from catching the horse in the first place.

Tugging the girth strap I scolded Bill under my breath. "Stop bloating your belly, horse!" Horses will often distend their belly when the saddle is tightened, likely to reduce discomfort. However, a loosened saddle is the result once an animal relaxes its breathing again. In the worstdisce instance this can endanger a rider. Putting my 120 pounds into it I yanked the strap upward. That is when Bill's head swung around. And his great teeth struck a fierce bite.

"Dang, Bill! Dang it!"

I leapt, swung at him and grabbed my side all at once. "Dumb Bill. Bad horse!"

The shock and sting let up after a minute. I lifted my shirt. An orange-red hue marked the area along his teeth marks. Thankfully the skin didn't break. "Dumb Bill."

Drawing parallels on human behavior came— I found afterward—more easily than I might have imagined. As in child-raising.

For instance, parents may, at times, place undue pressure on a child to conform. Discerning what helps both the child and the parent needs thoughtful consideration. Time, patience, and often, prayer.

In time I learned how to reduce undue pressure to a horse—and resulting teeth marks to my side. Spacing the cinch-tightenings with short walks between can relieve tensions and often settle the issue agreeably for horse and rider.

And being attentive. Likely, not so hard a thing to do, but being attentive must be done on purpose.

Noting body language, feelings, considering the horse's—or person's—point of view.

After the barnyard misunderstanding I always saddled Bill attentively. I kept one eye toward the girth strap, the other toward his head. Apparently, one can never be too careful dealing with a horse. Or a human.

CHAPTER NINE

DANCING WITH SNAKES

My only actual dance with a snake happened at the farm when I was around 12. Our horse, Bill, unknowingly played a role. Apart from the dance, I knew other reptile encounters growing up.

I was ten, enjoying a rare weekend family outing. We cabined at a clearing along the Neosho River.

"Come here you. Now stay put, little froggy."

I was fishing with a simple cane pole and line when the frog risked hopping into view. Threading it to my hook, I cast the line and waited for a fish to take in the new bait. Nothing.

Drawing the pole back, I brought in the line and the rig on the shore. The frog continued stirring. "I'll be back, frog." I moved beyond a tree for a potty break.

On my return, I puzzled at the scene. *Where's the hook, the sinker? Where's the frog?*

The far end of the fishing line no longer lay above the ground. It had vanished into a hole some feet away. Raising the cane pole, I felt resistance. Hoisting it higher, I caught my breath. From the hole in the ground rose the sinker—and, to my wonderment, a snake, busy swallowing my frog.

It was a bad day to be a frog, laboring to free itself from both a fish hook and a highly focused snake. Though the frog didn't survive, the serpent's day didn't end well, either. My brother Tim and I saw to it.

***

The dance was roughly two years later.

"Mom, I'm going for a ride on Bill."

As I entered tall Bermuda in a lower pasture, the Sunday afternoon was hot, heavy with humidity. I loved riding Old Bill. I loved less the effort required to catch him. Clever Bill knew when I carried horse tack —his halter, bridle, and bit. He liked his freedom and shrank from coming too close—swinging his long head away and loping off just as I clutched for his dark mane.

"Aw, Bill, you blamed creature!"

Sweaty and agitated after several failed attempts, I wound my arm and flung the tack his direction. A puff of dust lifted from dry earth as the gear landed, far short of the animal. Wiping my forehead, I shifted my hat. "Doggone, Bill." The horse had tested my resolve and had won. Today anyway.

Half-dejected, I trotted forward to retrieve the gear.

Unknown to me, a coiled snake lay silent in my path. It flew upward and around my right ankle the moment my boot landed nearby. The serpent spiraled up my blue jeans like a spirited corkscrew, swiftly circling around and around.

I shuddered and lurched. And danced. Wildly. The snake clung to my leg. "Ah-Ahh!-NAhh-AHH!!" I was never so panicked. Leaping on my left leg, I went kicking the right one down, outward, and back again the whole time. The fact that I leapt with my lame foot didn't matter a second. I must shake that thing free.

At last the snake released, dropped into the high grass and disappeared. I bolted several yards the opposite direction. I stopped to gather my breath. And composure.

In a sudden, embarrassing moment I realized that seconds ago I had lost it. Instinctively I glanced at my surroundings. Nothing but prairie grass and distant trees any direction. A short way off —grazing and disinterested—stood Bill. I was thankful for seclusion. And I was sheepish.

I retrieved the hardware and offered a silent pledge in the horse's direction. *Bill, you'll be in these next time.*

I started toward the barns, and to our house beyond.

I'll change from the moistened underwear, get tidied up. Mom will have lunch ready soon.

I relaxed. Altered my gait.

And almost smiled.

***

"And now we welcome two brothers—the Lout boys—to the waters of baptism." Our lady minister, dressed in white, smiling, beckoned my older brother and me. Sister Alva was standing in a cattle pond fifteen feet from shore.

The foreman of the ranch attended our church. In summer months he supplied this venue for those ready to be baptized.

Sister Alva adjusted her footing, steadying her bare feet on the pond's floor. She was waist deep, was poised, looking elegant. She noted our approach while pondering the dignity of her office. Considering her bearing, Sister Alva might as well be administering the sacrament in a cathedral.

Tim and I waded in. Our understanding of baptism's actual significance—at least my understanding—was limited, shallow as the waters hugging the pond bank. Our church didn't seem always to clarify some practices. To comply seemed the objective. Love God and do what the Bible says; Jesus was baptized by John, Jesus-followers get baptized. We're lowered into water and brought up again. Like Jesus in the Jordan.

This summed up our instruction on baptism for the most part, as I remember it. And, given we were Pentecostal, I vaguely caught that some people get the Holy Ghost at the moment of water baptism. Without irreverence I wondered. *Will I too talk in tongues when I come up for air?* Nearby, a mama cow bawled.

"OK, Tim," the minister counseled, "now squeeze your nose shut."

My brother complied. Facing him, Sister Alva placed her palm at his back, the other on his chest. She shut her eyes.

"Now, in the name of the Father and the Son and the Holy Ghost, I baptize you."

Invoking the divine titles she lowered Tim beneath the water and returned him upward. The small gathering of witnesses, our parents included, smiled their approval. The minister caught my eye and nodded. I stepped forward. The ritual was repeated.

I remember thinking this was a good thing that had been done to us. I also remember wishing we could remain longer —make further good use of the pond, swim around awhile.

Being baptized under the open sky in a setting familiar to a farm boy left me with a pleasant memory. My joy over the occasion, however, came years later. Wise and caring believers opened scriptures to me on the rich theme of water baptism. The beauty of identifying with Jesus. It was a belated joy but still a joy.

Tim and I brought our dripping bodies to shore. Our parents received us, mother extending a towel. We got into the family car, a '51 Ford.

Like passing from one room to another, our thoughts shifted from pasture and pond to mother's kitchen where a simmering oven roast surely waited.

Licking my lips, I recognized a taste—not a bad flavor, though different from what flowed through our kitchen faucet. Water from a special pond on a north county ranch.

We were therefore buried with him through baptism, in order that, just as Christ was raised from the dead. . . we too may live a new life.

-Romans 6

CHAPTER TEN

DISTRACTIVE BEHAVIOR

Distraction: That which divides the attention, diverts or draws away the mind; prevents concentration.

"Jerry Lout! What are you looking at out there? You come right up here."

Elementary school.

I limp through my life distracted. Not all the time.

But more of the time than desired. Ask my wife.

Occasionally my distractions serve a handy purpose. Even therapeutic. A quiet brook in a peaceful setting brings respite to a stressful day. Still, helpful distractions seem rare.

My inattention might have pinned a teenage chum under a tractor tire. I absent-mindedly left a fence-gate lying in my horse's pathway. Thankfully we cheated disaster. Still, distraction took me there.

"You come right up here, Jerry!"

My nine-year-old daydreaming mind had transported me outside our fourth grade classroom. The playground scene beyond the window had won me over. I surveyed a world beyond the smell of chalk dust and the warble of Mrs. Ballard's voice.

Whether the punishment fit the crime, her hard paddle stung. I quivered—from embarrassment as much as pain. My classmates hadn't often seen me blush or shed tears. They had a ringside seat today for both at the front of the room.

As with most kids, distractions peppered my growing-up years. Sidelined once by teenage infatuation I entered a covert alliance with a girl— and nearly train-wrecked my bond with my parents.

Motor vehicles and distractions don't do well together.

"Reckon we ought to move his motor-bike outa the street?"

My head throbbed. Lying face down, I struggled to make sense of the gentleman's folksy question.

I had been trying out the second-hand motorcycle dad had recently helped me buy.

Turning onto Sixth Street from Wood Drive I concentrated on my lame foot.

The bike's gears didn't respond well to the efforts of my left heel. Normally the gear is shifted by the shoe toe. But polio left me with no upward lift. So I improvised, directing my foot over and beyond the gear, and lifting the lever with the back of my heel. The tactic hampered the shift, brought distraction.

I looked up, and a car crossed before me from a side road. It was a safe distance away but its presence spooked me. I seized the front brake. It locked, tumbling me headlong. I wore no helmet.

My white and black Honda lay on its side. Strangers hauled me to a grassy spot off the street's edge, placing me face down. In some moments I stirred. Raising my head slightly I surveyed several pair of footwear facing me in a rough semicircle. At that point I heard the man's matter-of-fact query about my bike.

Gradually someone helped me up.

"Thank you." I could at least speak.

Another kind person steered me to a clinic, convenient steps nearby.

The doctor studied a place on my forehead.

"That's a real goose egg you have, young man."

He shined a light in each eye, shared a cautionary remark and sent me on my way. Days afterward I pondered some questions. Significant ones, I felt.

What Good Samaritan saw me to the clinic?

Who paid the doctor's visit (did anyone)?

Who retrieved my bike?

What mercy-givers hauled me out of harm's way and onto the grass?

What unseen force, presence, or hand kept the goose egg from cracking?

Thanksgiving welled up. Not to impersonal lucky stars.

Rather to one who—in faithfulness—attended to the inattentive. Delivered the distracted.

Next time I rode the helmet went on. I traded distraction for vigilance. For a while.

Sermons, like the odd bedtime prayer, helped scare me and unscare me from the scare.

Thankfully much of childhood church-life brought pleasure. We sang. Lots of singing. A few hymns and lots of simple, easy-to-follow Pentecostal choruses. Lusty, feeling-centered, singing. With few people paying attention to voice or instrument quality, all were free – to sway with rhythms and, in some measure, ponder lyrics. Foot tapping and handclapping and knee slapping often tipped the scale over gentler strains of music—reflective, contemplative . . . leave that style to the Presbyterians and Catholics and whomever. Instruments carried their non-negotiables. Without our available musical hardware of piano, guitars, and the occasional tambourine, church life might have proven barely durable.

It is not that good, soul-stirring preaching failed to happen. Much of whatever spiritual fervor may characterize my life can be traced to convictions, many of which formed in early church life. Some even moved me, the introvert kid, to now and then toss shyness out the door. David, an older gentleman, reflects.

"Jerry, how I remember that day . . . you limping clear back to where I sat at the end of a row during time of the altar call. You took my hand. You persuaded me to come on forward and surrender my life to God."

His eyes glisten, his smile broadens. "I will never forget that day I met salvation."

Church-sponsored vacation Bible school (VBS) every summer and Sunday school sessions met me in special   ways.

"Come on over here, Jerry. Near the flannel board. That's right. Now, take a look at these people, these animals and trees and such. Which one will you stick up on the board, Jerry?"

Hardly believing the teacher selected me with the honor, I stepped nearer.

"Yes, go ahead and pick it up," she coaxed.

I moved the shepherd figure with care to within a couple inches of a few sheep. A thrill passed through me.

***

"Mom, how many days until Robbers Cave?"

Summer kids camp at the state park flew by. We could hardly wait until next time. Our faith family and those of others in a loosely-knit network of independent Oklahoma churches gave, gave, and gave. Youth camp counselors, cooks, and clergy—workers doing what they did on sweltering summer days out of pure care for young ones. Supplying us heart touching times when my peers and I could rollick in the great outdoors and taste more of Jesus.

By the same token, lots of Sunday mornings, Sunday evenings, Tuesday evenings and Friday evenings (our expected times to be in God's House—a rule our household adhered to regardless how any given day had wearied my plumber dad). Lots of the teachings and preachings served up heavy helpings of shoulds.

"A Christian should read his Bible every day. You're a Christian, right? Good. You should do this. Praying Christians are real Christians—really praying Christians are really real Christians. You—we all—should pray. Really pray. Really."

So a weak area in my faith—in the understanding of faith—left me uncertain, insecure.

Learning to say right sayings and to perform my faith—rallying all my shoulds, to do so—became the goal. Any conscious notion that I actually pursued goals in this way escaped me. I didn't think of it. Just knew I should.

When revival preachers came through, they brought big Bibles, impressive wardrobes, hell-fire sermons (especially in the earlier years), and plenty of handkerchiefs. For the sweat.

My father labored in the plumbing craft. Plumbers know how to sweat. From dad's face, his neck and arms, from the back and the front of his work shirt poured sweat. Ever-present moisture in generous amounts—more of it in July and August. Yet, from my blue-collar dad perspiration never flowed more freely nor fully than sweat pouring from the white-collared neck of our revival evangelists. Especially Brother Mozden. Regardless how cool the sanctuary, only a few minutes passed in the message before his hanky came out—breezed fully open by a flick of his wrist. The pocket from which it was drawn did not see the hanky again until the sermon ended.

I liked his preaching. I am sure some of this was because of the Holy Spirit using Rev. Mozden's Bible messages to get me tighter with God. But I think, too, his preaching drew me like a scary movie does. Scaring the bejeebers out of you and holding out hope of a good ending. Which usually came.

Revival meetings always seemed best on the fourth or fifth night. Revival meant week-long nightly meetings with an out-of-town preacher delivering fearfully graphic sermons on fiery punishments of sinners. Some sermons may have covered other topics. I remember this variety most. I felt so unholy by those closing nights I knew I must visit the altar another time and make sure I was ready to meet judgment if I died in my sleep or in a crashing car.

If my conscience happened to relax or lay dormant over a season, it rallied most in times of religious meetings—and most keenly during revival week, when my heart pounded fearfully over the more graphic images of hell.

"Don't squeeze too hard, son." I was near age six, seated by my dad and snuggling as close as possible against his right side. His arm rested on the bench pew behind my head, allowing his hand to hang within reach. A red-costumed devil displaying horns, slanted eyes, and forked tail, screeched to an actor holding a beer. "YES. Now I have you. You are mine. Mine." The devil had seized the man. Holding a firm grip on the sinner, Satan swung his gaze toward the audience. I knew he was charging for me any minute. Turning again to his captive he dragged the despairing man toward a make-shift divider on stage. Screams of pain rose from other victims in the back of the divider—where lay the Lake of Fire. I gripped my father's thumb until it lost feeling.

Snapshots like these are simply that. In all the growing-up years I knew in our little church—among warm, generous, sacrificial, all-out-for-Jesus, people—my heritage is more than rich.

Faith is a journey. Over time I discovered God's grace. Grace had a presence in our congregation, no question. But I stayed for the most part tenuous, insecure in my believing identity. Little able to detect or recognize grace—or enter the joyful, growing-up living it brings. Little by little Jesus' grace began leading me to a place fuller, richer than the land of Should. But not yet. For now,

Save me again, Jesus.

CHAPTER ELEVEN

UNDER THE INFLUENCE

Three brothers of one family believed in me. Each played an influencing role in my life. Each introduced me to something or someone—marking me for life. For good. I'm in their debt.

The Creason brothers were common men of uncommon influence. Troy and Melvin impacted me first.

Troy (small business-owner, cattle-tender)

Troy sat with 11- and 12-year-old boys in a tight, windowless room. On our straight-back chairs and short benches, we boys formed a square with most of our backs touching a wall. Ricky, Larry, Dwight, Tim, James. Afterward, Dennis, Steve, another Tim...

Brother Troy's King James Bible lay open before him. With a calloused forefinger he tracked the sentences as he read. His instruction in down-to-earth terms supplied me and the others with building blocks of truth. For life. Though we may have retained only a trace of the riches dispensed, Troy showed up week by week.

What he shared, he lived. The truths could bring us into and through a meaningful life. He knew this. He introduced us to Christ: his nature and character; truthfulness, perseverance, responsibility, faith. A life with Jesus was the life to live. Nothing else made sense. I never doubted Troy's motives, his reasons for showing up. Why would I? The reason was obvious. He believed the book. He believed in us.

Melvin (farmer, welder)

Melvin wowed me as a youth leader. He and his auburn-haired wife, Joan, endeared themselves to the teens.

Melvin was never splashy, sensational. But engaging, sincere. Attentive. If in my teen years I relished anything to do with church it was tied to Melvin.

"Brother Melvin, could you teach me to make a necktie knot?"

"Sure. Just a second. I'll adjust this mirror."

The white Ford Mustang breezed along Highway 75—Melvin and his wife up front. We were off to a Monday night youth rally. I sat squeezed between other students in the back seat, positioning my Adam's apple to meet Melvin's focus through his rearview mirror.

My clumsy fingers fumbled with a knot-in-progress as Melvin —steering wheel firmly in hand— talked me through.

"OK Jerry, thread the broad part over, then under and through (pause); now up and out the triangular opening, then . . ."

Melvin glanced first to the mirror, then to the road and back again. This two-step rumba continued, alternating between the highway and my knot-tying exercise. He patiently took me through the steps, assuring me along the way. Melvin believed in me.

I would get this knot tied. I knew it.

I heard a piece of wisdom years after my evening along Highway 75: "If you hold rich memories of some person who made a positive influence in your life be assured—that person was an encourager." The experience—one in a long list of happenings with Melvin—illustrated the truth.

Be a blessing.

Youth Pastor Melvin personified this tender mandate of scripture. He blessed—by his personal devotion, by his belief in us, his young charges. Influencing us into the future.

When our 35th anniversary came, Ann and I renewed our marriage vows at the little church, where my family had worshiped, where the two of us were wed.

As I dressed for the affair I threaded my green and white tie. Snugged the knot securely. Melvin would officiate our milestone renewal. I reviewed my workmanship and smiled.

Will he notice the knot?

***

Sometimes lessons are slow in coming.

My eyes pooled with tears. A crinkled paper bearing rhythmic lines lay open on the administrator's desk between us.

He was an imposing man, Mr. B.

His bearing when wielding a paddle, which I knew to beconcealed somewhere in this room, provoked dread.

Still, my sorrow rose from a sting greater than the approaching whoosh of a board. My offense was serious. Worse than serious. Shameful. Remorse brought on the tears.

The irony was the instruments I had used to inflict pain. Not rocks shattering a classroom window. Not matches igniting a chemistry lab. Nothing menacing that way. A simple writing pad and ballpoint pen.

Now I was here in Mr. B's office.

I sat silent across from him, hands on my lap, reflecting the ugliness of my deed. No teacher deserved the mockery I scrawled on that paper. Not this one. Not any. A tear landed on my right thumb.

The teacher had become, over time, the object of whispered jokes by several students. Amused, I crafted a poem—humor of the worst kind—demeaning.

I was as dumb as my act was unkind—signing my name and passing it to a friend. He read it, grinned and passed it to another student.

I didn't see my work of poetry again. Until now, two days later, when called to Mr. B's office. There it lay on his desk. After blubbering my apology I bent forward and gripped my ankles. Whack. Whack. Whack. Whack.

While other means may be preferred to bring home hard lessons, the fierce sting of a seasoned paddle proved reasonably effective for one high school boy.

***

In battered tennis shoes we shuffled through leaves of gold and red. A wooded area on his family's land. Kenny pointed to a brown clump of dead vines gracing a tree stump. End-of-summer rains hadn't arrived and we easily crossed the creek bed to reach them. I grinned.

Our September birthdays fell within a day of each other though we were three years apart. I was the older.

"Yeah, these oughta smoke well."

A few pocket knife moves and we were set. I touched a lighted match to our smokes. We inhaled. And instantly discerned how greatly overrated the vine-smoking thrill was. Tears blocked our vision. We gagged on acrid smoke. The coughing trailed off in time.

Kenny and I did what country kids did in the 1950s. Some things, like inhaling fiery toxins, could have injured us. Badly. Surviving childhood itself was indeed a notable feat, as my experiences, especially with Kenny, can give witness to.

Perched behind me beyond the saddle, Kenny was suddenly propelled to the grassy roadside as a passing semi spooked our horse.

Another time, towing the harrow (farm implement for smoothing broken sod) I swung the tractor too sharply into a turn.

"Look out, Jerry. It's coming down on us!"

A big tire caught the harrow's edge, shooting it upward. Falling again, a metal bar pinned Kenny's shoe to the tractor's axle casing on which he stood. His foot barely escaped. I pried the empty shoe out and offered it to him silently.

Dodging BBs zinging from each other's Daisy rifles. Years later we realized we both had won all the contests—finishing the shootouts with our eyesight still intact.

My friend Kenny and I jumped from roof sheds. We swam in snake-colonized ponds, fished for crawdads with bacon bits. And lit up discarded Marlboros we randomly happened upon. As we got a little older our common love of music grew.

***

"Tim", I whispered to my brother, "scoot your chair back just an inch so I can see Brother Elmer's chording. The church guitarist, happily made room for us, his unofficial young apprentices. Our hunger to master the instrument emboldened us to ascend the church platform, even for Sunday meetings, taking our positions to Brother Elmer's right. From this angle we could mimic his fingering moves and strum along in toe-tapping rhythms. Afterward, back home, my brother and I devoted hour on hour to the cause. We grew as proud of our calloused fingertips as we were of our, slick-backed, Brylcreem hair.

With my brother Tim taking the lead plus the obvious aid of our Sunday meeting mentor, we each picked up the basics of guitar—devoting hour on hour to its mastery. Soon Kenny joined in. We formed our own singing group with three-part harmony, even naming ourselves, Sons of Faith. What fun. Singing at the Living Way and a handful of other small-town gatherings.

"Hey, have you heard that new guy, David, play? Man alive."

We assigned David lead guitarist. He wrecked a night of sleep for the team on one of our little road trips. By talking in his sleep.

"Fellas, can you come sing for us next Saturday?"

The weekend came. We loaded up our sparse equipment and set out for Wetumka.

The host guided our team to the sleeping quarters after the evening of picking and singing ended. "Make yourselves at home, fellas. The bathroom's through that door."

Five twin beds lay at odd angles, filling up the small room and leaving little space to move about.

David, groggy from a busy week and our night of music followed by burgers and fries our hosts fed us, stretched out face down on a bed. The rest of us were soon a captive audience to his nonstop ramblings. We saw he was sound asleep. We listened, staring, realizing that—until this moment—none of us had ever encountered a sleep talker in action. David's animated blabber went on, leaving us more entertained by the moment. One of the boys suddenly spoke up in a low but excited voice.

"Fellas, I got an idea. . . let's each grab a corner of David—you know, one at each shoulder, one at each leg. . ."

"Yeah, I get it", another boy added, his eyes widening. "He's on his belly. We count to three, pick him up slowly and move him to an empty bed. . . is that the idea?"

We moved toward our unsuspecting lead guitarist.

With each boy taking a gentle but firm grip, we counted to three, our lips in synch as in a shared pantomime.

Raising him, we moved slowly backward, carrying him feet-first toward the waiting mattress.

Still fully asleep but now growing restless, David quickly changed his droning monologue and his body stirred to action.

As in a frantic, forward-swimming motion, he labored against our pull, sensing a force stealing him off to another place. We staggered—partly in trying to offset his resistance, partly from our silent, heaving laughter.

More agitated still, David called out, laboring against our restraints, working harder than ever to "paddle" forward. His sleeping voice went louder.

"No, no! Don't—don't flush it! No, Don't Flush It!". It was here we nearly dropped him, overcome by the absurd image seizing our minds. We lowered him safely at last and he soon fell into deep slumber. Sleep for the rest of us, on the other hand was delayed a while. A soft chuckle would rise in the darkened room, triggering yet another ripple of laughs.

The morning tap on our door and call to breakfast came far too soon for everyone.

Except, perhaps, for David. He had not wakened once.

***

Kenny. The funnest guy I knew. Quick wit. Contagious smile. Musical.

He soaked up kindness, wherever he found it. Like a sponge.

Kenny limped. Not physically.

Alcohol, it could be said, cheated him of youth—at least to a measure.

Misuse of liquor. Not his. Not yet.

In several ways, Kenny still displayed not poverty—but richness.

Rich in personal charm, he prospered otherwise in big-heartedness—having opened himself early to heaven's large-hearted father. He knew wealth of spirit—a treasure, to him, inaccessible elsewhere.

But Kenny knew scarcity.

Kenny's family suffered lack through an absentee parent, a limping parent. Absent emotionally, often physically. Family dependents struggled to get by while resources of the home's wage-earner fed an addiction.

It's been said that alcohol abuse impoverishes the brain. One could add: and people.

"I'm off to California, friend."

Kenny's talents opened for him a new world in the coastal state. To a music label, in time—an on-ramp to fame. For a season.

Kenny was offered a drink by a religious leader he admired. The drink led to another. He spiraled.

Years afterward, adrift on a California freeway, my awesome and hurting childhood friend met with fear. Then, something else.

"I tried to navigate the freeway in my beat-up Volkswagen. Empty beer cans covered the floor all around. I leaned to the center mirror. My eyes met their own gaze. And fear hit me full force.

"Who is that person? I didn't recognize myself. I was so frightened. And I knew. It's time.

"Taking an exit I drove to the home of a man I had known. A believer in Jesus."

Kenny's freeway exit became his entry ramp. To his old acquaintance. To a twelve step group. To hope. To sobriety. Then, to service.

Visiting a jail or prison today you might find Kenny—guitar in hand, his infectious smile. From Arizona to California, to Oklahoma to Florida.

Kenny's name is known. He is welcome. Every time, among the lame ones who are overly-acquainted with their limps.

He speaks to men's hearts. Not as outsider but as peer. They warm to him. His quick wit, his songs and his story. A long-time apprentice of Jesus, Kenny's their friend. Fellow-traveler. Limping. He has led some of the men through recovery steps. He's led some to counselling sessions. Others to confession. All toward Jesus.

A guard unlocks and relocks gates as Kenny moves further inside. He takes a place nearby and unlatches his guitar case. Incarcerated men glimpse him. Some know him and they smile.

Kenny himself has warmed to the gathering well before arriving.

He takes up his instrument and breaks out in a fun impersonation, "Anybody heard of Johnny Cash?"

Hands clap in rhythm. More smiles meet his.

Those acquainted with the program are happy for the ice-breaking music. Their vision, though, is trained to the table near his guitar case.

It's there. The book. Kenny's Bible.

He'll shift to "The Old Rugged Cross" and other hymns soon, several prisoners predict silently. One leans back, inhales long—like welcoming an aroma. Humming to the rhythms, he regards the small table again.

Brother Kenny's here today. With the book. Today is a good day.

Beauty instead of ashes, the oil of joy instead of mourning, and a garment of praise instead of a spirit of despair.   – Isaiah 61

***

The distance separating our hogs from our rabbits was 50 yards by measuring tape—light years by culture. Pigs, nasty and unique. For a boy assigned feeding them, they're both annoying and amusing.

With no real purpose to stay, I stuck around after slopping them simply to hear their throaty grunts and grin at their antics—rubbery flat noses shoveling mud, curly tails twitching like a drum major's out of rhythm baton.

Slop the hogs. A more refined expression, *feed the hogs*, might have elevated the task's dignity. Then again, they were hogs. My knee took a sharp thud.

"Stupid sow.

"Patient, be patient, pig! No slamming against the fence there."

Raising an over-full bucket of pig slop above the wood-slat enclosure demanded focus and balance—neither of which I won awards for. It was worse when the pig family was extra-eager for dinner. More than once my boots or a swath of blue jeans got sloshed with the drippy, sweet-and-sour brew.

Leftovers from most meals helped fashion the recipe. "Be sure the pigs get these leftovers," mom called. Potato skins, half-eaten apples, tomato bits, stale or fresh bread. Finally, barley or oat seed blended with water made up the rest.

"Here Tim," I called—a pail swinging at my knee. "Mom wants these water melon rinds in, too."

**

At certain seasons rifle shots in any wooded area means a squirrel is wise to take cover.

"Help. Help! Uh, somebody?" I fought an approaching panic. "Help!" I was easily of age to climb trees—just not while bearing firearms. Once up the tree, I struggled to make my descent without discharging the .22 rifle I carried.

"Now just what are you doing up there, Jerry Lout?"

Neighbor Bill, a mischievous glint in his eye, craned his neck. He clearly enjoyed my plight, choosing to linger more than necessary with general chitchat before seeing the gun and me safely to the ground. I thanked him briskly and trudged toward home. Bill's good-natured chuckle echoed in my ears for days. Good neighbors peppered Oklahoma's rural landscape, mutually subscribing to unwritten codes of honorable conduct.

160

***

"Mr. Lout. I just gotta' say, Mr. Lout, that boy o' yours. He know how to shoot. Me, I never ever see a grown man shoot a gun like that boy. He know how to shoot!"

Willie, the diligent part-time worker our dad employed, made much of my marksmanship. In truth, I could not boast a trace of such talent and knew it. With a shotgun. . . maybe. Never with a small rifle. No way. Lucky, that's what I was—plumb lucky.

I'd stood in a broad grazing area beyond our south barn when the cotton tail darted from a thick grassy patch. It bounded across the field. Bringing the rifle up, I followed its springing movement and fired. The rabbit dropped, a head shot.

Willie's assessment never mellowed. He'd witnessed a first-class sharpshooter in action. Privately I reveled in the fantasy, grinning into the next day.

Someone thinks I'm really good. Well, for a day I'll just believe it, too.

***

The north pond.

With its home-made diving board—thanks to our dad's heart for his boy's summer merriment—the north pond supplied a coveted recess from mid-summer heat.

Several cattle, belly-deep in the waters, grudgingly shared our private pool with its brown surface and squishy floor. They lumbered out as we waded in. Seconds later we two brothers and any pals along launched our routine mud-fight. Like most farm kids we knew the pond was short on sanitation. And like them, we didn't care.

"No fair, Larry!" Tim laughed. "That mud-ball you hit me with? It wasn't just mud."

***

If summertime meant pond time, so did an occasional cooler season.

"I'll beat you in!" Darren shouted.

Shedding a stocking here, a shirt there—running forward the whole time—peeling off more garments until not a stich remained, my pal splashed into the water ahead of me. While I, with my better leg first, then the other—danced myself bare. Shivering.

Not patient enough to await a summertime dip—meaning actual climate relief, our spur-of-the-moment skinny-dip in March chilled us to the bone. The escape we made from the pond passed as quickly as our entry into it.

Rapidly re-dressing, I called out, "Lucky the tree grove and barn blocked us from highway view."

And lucky indeed for any motorists travelling the route.

***

"Clear across, clear across!" we chanted. Excited shouts lifted to a wintry sky. Our bundled up ragtag crew thrilled at breezing across the pond. Challenging, counter-challenging, "Go, go, go!"

Years afterward, I wondered at our parents' trust. Granting me command of a motorized vehicle after nearly tumbling one into a creek bed. Trusting my brother and me to swim in questionable waters after my near-disastrous dive that might have brought a neck fracture. And a big puzzlement—trusting our sliding around frozen cattle ponds. Not for a moment have I regretted their trust, or even questioned their judgment. I only wondered at it. And thanked the Almighty for additionally assigned angels he dispatched.

A pond our cattle drank from froze over several times each winter the ice thick enough to bear the weight of an adolescent boy. Or two. Or three.

Taking a run toward the pond's near edge from a good distance away—negotiating frozen dirt clods and corn stalk remnants along the way—was a thrill. Speed gathered, a pair of leather-soled shoes connected on a glazed surface, and then the boy squatted or leaned in, depending his strategy. And then he glided as far as a person of that weight and velocity might warrant.

"Guys, I doubt we should try it today. It's getting a little mushy along the shore." We used what judgment growing children might employ. And somehow we survived.

Some of the best, and at times scariest—sounds of cracking ice can terrify—memories ever. Finally, compelled by encroaching nightfall or threat of frostbite, we surrendered the day and headed home. Our tingling cold nostrils savored the aroma of hot chocolate well before we reached the door.

The passing of time brought an inevitable thaw but young, thrill-seeking minds never lacked for creativity.

"Hey, grab that cardboard, I've got mine." Tim and I, along with our buddies, careened down grassy slopes on the exterior side of pond banks. Taking turns, we perched on and clung to remnants of cardboard, their undersides smoothed by repeated toboggan-like runs over flattened grass. We breezed downward with speeds we suspected might outdo alpine skiers.

**

My heart sank—as if actually mimicking my dad's car—which was now lowering itself axle-deep in mud.

The image of an overturned pickup of a time not long ago revisited my mind. I tapped the Olds 88 steering wheel. Really? Sharp Road? Again?

"Mm, sorry about this," I muttered to my Saturday night date.

"Keep the doors locked. I'll be back soon." I set out in the direction from which we'd driven—westward on Highway 56.

Keeping to small-town date-night ritual, we had done a casual roundtrip drive to the lake. En route back to town I had forgotten the heavy rains of the past few days and swung the vehicle onto unpaved Sharp Road. Now I bemoaned my error.

How do I get myself into these jams?

The uneven clip-thump of my shoe soles sank into rhythm with a cricket and frog band serenading the night.

Eyeing a farm-house light beyond a thick wooded area, I crossed a barbed-wire fence and squished through dark, rain-soaked pastureland. I whispered, "Don't let mean dogs or an old bull come after me before I reach that light."

The silhouette of an old tractor—looks like a Ford—offered some hope.

Well, here goes. Lord, let him be a friendly farmer. I stood a distance from the house but well enough inside a clearing where I could be seen.

Here goes.

My strongest voice stirred as I silently pleaded, *Please, God. No dogs.*

"Hello! Hello. Anyone at home? Hello!"

When the only barking sound came from a distant neighbor's place, I gave a grateful sigh. A screen door screeched and a medium-built man stepped onto the elevated porch. I could see his head protrude forward and imagined a pair of squinting eyes. I took advantage of the momentary quiet.

"Sir, I'm over here. I'm real sorry to bother you, sir. My car got stuck over there at the Sharp Road junction." I pointlessly waved my arm toward the road. "I wonder if you might be able to help?"

His lingering pause ended. "Hold on a minute."

The man turned and sent a short message to someone indoors. His knee-high rubber boots in place, he moved toward the tractor. Whew, I breathed.

A chain rattled as he wrapped it around the tractor's draw bar. We chugged to the crippled Oldsmobile, few words passing between us.

More chain sounds as he hooked a link to the car's frame. Seconds later the tractor belched. It edged forward, coaxing the heavy car backward and out of the bog.

"There, that's got it." Brushing his palms together, the satisfied gentleman signaled his triumph. A chunk of mud dropped from his coveralled knee cap.

"Thanks a lot, sir."

He touched his cap bill, acknowledging my date. "You all be careful."

I transported the girl, who had displayed a lot of patience, on to her home. Later, at my own place, I wasted no time taking up a water hose and old towel.

I notified my dad before graduating college.

***

Our father seldom voiced any personal wants. I recall a rare exception.

"Boys, my fiftieth birthday is coming next month." Tim and I shared a quick glance between us.

As a gift from you two, I think I'd like you to start calling me Dad. Instead of "Daddy."

It seemed to me in that moment all three of us became just a little more manly. But I was in for more growing pains. I little knew how soon.

CHAPTER TWELVE

REMEDIAL MEASURES

I fell hard for a girl. A young woman really.

I was too immature. Too naïve. Too much of a romantic. And too headstrong.

Sue was too attractive, too innocent. Too married.

Yes. Separated from her spouse in another state. Married.

Sue was nearly 20. I was 16 and just out of 11th grade.

To her credit, Sue did not initiate the romance—nor encourage it. Not strongly.

Still, our affections for each other grew.

My parents tried advising me. I was headstrong but I didn't think so, in love and "knew" so. My parents tried boundaries. I ignored them. They warned. I dug in. Stopping short of direct surveillance, my mother and father grew more attentive to my movements.

So I schemed.

I'll just walk the two miles to her place after lights out. Visit with her awhile, then walk back.

My schemings were short-lived.

Poets say love is blind. I proved them true by forgetting how visible a horse is.

"Jerry, I have one question." It was late afternoon—several weeks into my ruse. My father's confronting tone ruffled me. He continued.

"I saw Bill tethered today in front of Sue's grandmother's place."

Trouble lay ahead. How could I have been so dumb?

I had secured Bill's bridle reins to a tree in front of the grandma's house. Along a route my dad regularly drove.

"You were there, weren't you?" he challenged. "With Sue?" I bristled at the accusing edge in my father's voice. *This isn't fair*, I thought sullenly.

I didn't reply and, though I knew better, I returned his glare. My brand of love was moving from blind to deranged. Dad's fingers slid along his leather belt. My thoughts flew to other encounters.

A year or two earlier I had gotten ticked off when called on to mow the lawn. Though I was outside, my dad, through a window, read my lips as a cuss word left them. In seconds his belt found my backside. Memories evoked by his fingering the leather were of this sort—not ending well.

My 17th birthday arrived, and then passed, with little regard and no celebration. After our standoff, a cloudy mood seemed to settle in. My good-hearted parents felt more grief than indignation. They prayed. They surely discussed together.

Some things simply call for preventive medicine—extra strength. The hard decision was made. I was actually thankful to go away. From here—even from the girl-woman—for a while. My parents and I reached an accord.

One autumn morning I boarded a bus for another state. I would go to my sister's home. I glimpsed out toward my mother and father. Standing there together, they looked glum. Tired. A feeling of sadness encroached. I turned my face to the seat before me and turned my thoughts to anything I could.

Where will this take me, this time in Denver?

***

Thirty years after my mother's California bus journeys I took the same line toward Colorado's Rockies. I rode past giant grain elevators of Enid where nearly half of Oklahoma's harvested wheat is kept. In other conditions, my trip might have been an adventure. The bus passed through towns of romantic, historic, sometimes fanciful, names. Stillwater. Fort Supply. Slapout. At seventeen I had never travelled alone, nor with strangers, farther than about six miles from my home.

Melancholy. Adventure. Tension. The feelings mingled with others. Back home at Preston High my 20-or-so class-mates navigated two modest hallways. Now I neared, with each passing fencepost, a school that would dwarf any I had ever seen. Greater Denver's population numbered more than half my state. What's a big school like anyway? For a rural outsider, going to 12th grade?

I suspect my father's uncommon measure of sending me off rose largely from fear. Tensions, frustrations, awareness of his own short fuse. He couldn't risk injuring our relationship further by keeping me close by. Not for now.

This distance may be a safer, even more healing choice—if healing would, indeed, happen. He could take comfort, too, that I'd be in good hands with his daughter, my sister Betty. He knew her to be responsible.

In 1962 fewer than 500 McDonald's restaurants served North America. I entered school right away and took a weekend job at the Golden Arches. I served up 15-cent fries with 15-cent burgers. Colorado introduced me to pepperoni pizza, moisture-starved nasal passages from a mile-high climate, and the Cuban Missile Crisis. TV viewers were drilled often with contingency plans, with looping announcements running each day.

"All traffic lanes will change to one-way," the T.V. anchor intoned, "taking motorists outward— away from the metro area should evacuation sirens sound." The environment was tense. The crisis passed.

Somehow in spite of her own struggles at the time, my sis stepped up. Supplying, in random interchanges, perspectives, tidbits of wisdom. She dispensed common sense which, until now had been anything but common in her kid brother's head. Asking God's help, Betty cut through confused tangles of my unsound thinking. Light started seeping in. Threads of understanding.

Months in, I received word that my heart-throb had left my state. Somehow I traced a number to Sue and rang it.

"Hello."

A flat male voice answered. I was standing. My back brushed the kitchen wall. Finding my voice, I asked.

"May I speak with Sue?"

The man's voice went silent. After some seconds she took up the phone.

"Hello."

"Sue, have you gone back to your home—in your own state?"

"Yes."

"Does this mean . . . things are over now?"

"Yes." She paused. "I need to go now. Goodbye."

Concise. Surgical. As with a swift amputation—but lacking anesthetic.

Hardly attuned to my kitchen surroundings, I unraveled, unable or unwilling to mask emotion. I was a wreck—a heap of pre-twenties hormones, misapplied affections. Conflicted.

The wreck slid down the wall. Not having really sorrowed for a good while —probable mark of a callousing heart—I let flow a torrent. After minutes, when the sobs waned, I was spent. Breathing in a long sigh, I took in my surroundings. The space was still mine alone.

More clearness of thinking surfaced. Tears resumed—this time washing tears.

Truth seemed to find a footing inside. Like a homesick reject coming back after a long absence. What irony. I softened further and looked upward.

Father. Father.

I am so sorry. Tears again.

Added words didn't seem needed, or expected. I sensed the Shepherd God wasn't after a homily, a prayer as such. Just my heart. Responding to grace. To him.

A deep quiet followed. I savored it a while. Thankfully. Really thankful.

Home. The word came as a silent whisper inside. Then repeating itself.

My lame foot had gone to sleep from its place under me on the floor. I rotated it a little. It stirred. I drew myself up and reached again for the wall-mounted green phone.

"Yes, ma'am. I need to make a call." Soon a familiar voice was on the line.

"Dad?"

"Yes."

"I'd like to come home."

"Your mother and I are here, Son."

I never knew a better Christmas.

He will turn the hearts of the parents to their children, and the hearts of the children to their parents.

- Malachi 4

CHAPTER THIRTEEN

FEET and FACES

"All right everybody. It's that time."

Though the sanctuary lighting was nothing exceptional, it highlighted the richest shock of blond hair I had ever seen on anyone, male or female. The occasion—our youth rally, where teens showed up at the gathering's host church, wherever it happened to be that month.

Oddly, for a clergy simply receiving an offering Pastor John's enthusiasm seemed tangible. Contagious. The glint in his blue eyes conveyed his pleasure. And warmth. This was near his heart —this offering for missions.

Songs had already been sung. Hands had clapped. Youthful energy released into guitar strings, accordion keys, and the occasional tambourine. It was the way with our youth rallies. Kids with musical talent—whether well developed or barely evolving— united in praise. John affirmed at every level. No spectator himself, his own electric guitar drooped comfortably at his midsection. It responded easily to his touch.

Two empty collection baskets sat at the church's altar up front.

"OK, here's our chance to join the Lord in sending his Good News of Jesus throughout the world." He went on, the contagious smile strong as ever.

"Our rally offerings help Nigerian evangelists share Jesus way over there in Africa. But now first, young people (his voice softened), let's quiet ourselves. Let's pray for our dear brothers laboring in hard places far from here. These servants need our prayers as much as our quarters, dimes and dollars."

By the prayer's ending most of us guys and girls fished what currency we could from our blue-jean pockets or pink and silver purses.

Filing from our seats, weaving forward, we dropped our modest offerings in the baskets, confidently dispatching salvation to the ends of the earth.

Pastor John laid aside a guitar pick. He took up his microphone, then his Bible, soon finding a reference.

"Young people, listen up. I want you to hear this. Tonight we are helping African brothers to go among their own—taking God's precious message of hope and life."

"Listen." The slight pastor with his planet-size heart paused reverently. The room quieted.

"God calls every one of us to the mission field in one way or the other, all of us to the world's unreached nations. Now. I want you to do something. Turn your eyes toward your shoes. Just do this, would you. Look at your shoes now, your feet. Keep your eyes to them."

Our focus shifted from hair-dos, from after-meeting burgers and fries, and from wherever our minds may have been carried by a random daydream.

Pastor John read from his Bible, his tone deliberate. We, his youthful audience stood quietly. Our eyes attentive, throughout the chapel, on our own pair of feet.

"How beautiful are the feet of those that bring good news!" – Romans 10

I stared at the pair of shoes nearest me. My own. The shoe at the end of my shorter leg—the limping one—sometimes tripped. My mind went to descriptive mode.

Shoes. Home to the weirdest, most pitiful-looking feet in the county—maybe state?

Then, in curious mood, I found myself asking a *what if* question.

What if, in God's eyes somehow—what if he sees beauty? Even in this pair of feet?

I smiled slightly. In the continued quiet supplied by an unhurried Pastor John, the question surfaced again. From within. More forcefully, but sweetly. *What if.*

What if?

I felt my eyes moisten. As if to water a seed.

***

"I see black faces."

Reverend Alva, our lady minister, signaled me with a compassionate but direct look. It was Sunday evening worship time in Okmulgee. I had entered my last semester of high school.

"Jerry, many of them are gathered," she continued. "A sea of black faces. You are standing before them. Speaking to them. I'm not sure what it may mean. But I see this."

Her eyes and voice conveyed certainty. Rev. Alva was confident of what had met her vision.

Vision. Rev. Alva saw a vision—at least a mental impression—with me in it?

I thought of the picture's content—tried imagining the scene. My response was respectful silence. No goose bumps or chills. Still I knew from my heritage that these kinds of things can carry meaning. *Maybe there is a scent of something here I will connect with further down the road. Maybe not.* I shelved the message of the vision, asking the Lord to do his will.

Weeks later green buds started showing on trees. Leaves emerged, flowers revived. With them, spring colors. Senior commencement drew nearer. I fell into a reflective mood—calling to mind people and events intersecting my life up to the present.

A leg brace, pear-tree climbing with Tim, Opaline and VBS, mischief, a polio ward, hayfields, heartbreak, home . . . And youth rallies with friends— Billy, Marilyn, James, Pat. . .

Musings continued.

From age five I sang lustily on Lord's Day. Up front in the sanctuary with my peers. A happy routine each week—us all in a line across the front. Just before dispersing to our Sunday School classes.

This little light of mine, I'm gonna let it shine. . . Deep and wide, deep and wide; there's a fountain flowing deep and wide. . . Zacchaeus was a wee little man, a wee little man was he. . .

I drew a handkerchief from my back left pocket and tooted my nose, telling myself it was seasonal sinus.

The reflective mood carried me deeper, to feelings beyond simple nostalgia. Shortly, another tune surfaced. I had learned it at youth rally. And we sang it at Robbers Cave Park Camps. The lyrics came easily. I smiled, remembering its first attempt among us. Led by wavy-haired Pastor John.

It may not be on the mountain's height
Or over the stormy sea;
It may not be at the battle's front
my Lord will have need of me;
But if by a still, small voice He calls
to paths that I do not know,
I'll answer, dear Lord, with my hand in Thine,
I'll go where You want me to go.
I'll go where You want me to go, dear Lord,
O'er mountain, or plain, or sea;
I'll say what You want me to say, dear Lord,
I'll be what You want me to be.

The song stirred memories. Feelings. Of gathered teens at the front of campground chapels and church auditoriums. Singing the prayer, but also praying the song.

Church ministers sometimes labeled things. Helping us tune ourselves to movings, stirrings of spirit. Our teen faces often moistened by the song's last stanza . . . tears of consecration.

Sensing the tender presence I again fished out my handkerchief. I grew thoughtful. An image of some months ago visited my mind.

Of distant lands. Of black faces.

***

"Did you hear the president's been shot?"

During several high school summers —when not bailing hay with him—I helped Dad in his small business. At City Plumbing my duties featured grunts, grime, and unmentionable substances. Dodging spiders in under-house crawl spaces I soaped up fitting joints along black pipe gas lines. Bubbling up of liquid detergent applied by paintbrush around the joints revealed any leaks. I threaded galvanized pipe and maneuvered flat steel rods (snakes) along clogged restaurant sewer lines. My before-dinner hand scrubbing redefined the term *ferocity.*

My Preston High years behind me, a construction firm hired both my father and me in late summer. As plumber's apprentice I shadowed my journeyman dad, gaining experience in the trade. We were on a team renovating Okmulgee's post office building. I sniffed the bunker-like quarters. Blended smells of concrete, sawdust and dankness indicated our basement environment. Carpenters, electricians, plumbers, playing their roles in a tradesmen's symphony.

November 22, 1963

The basement elevator door opened to my dad and me. It was midday. We would surface to first floor and take to our charcoal-black lunch pails. The kind with contoured lids harboring a thermos. Dad responded to the terse question about the president.

"No, what about it?"

I dusted my work cap. Dad waited for a punch line to the man's unsavory joke. It didn't come.

"It's not a joke, Clyde."

That Friday our lunch pails lost their appeal as our transport hauled us upward. The elevator scene found permanent residence in a newly-fashioned file in my brain.

Years later the writings of a gifted Oxford professor captured my imagination. I would rate the Irishman —who died the same day as President Kennedy—among my favorite authors. C. S. Lewis.

I believe we all have a limp, perhaps more than one. What manner of crippling could so wreck a person's mind to make him become a murderer? Of America's 35th president?

I worked with dad throughout the post office project. Over time I knew. The plumbing trade isn't for me. I just wasn't suited for it. Dad's work was an honorable vocation. For me, the sensation of typewriter keys clicking under my fingertips felt more at home than the imprint of a pipe wrench on my palm.

Preston High had provided me time in the company of names like Royal and Underwood. I loved the forming of words . . . of thoughts transmitted to paper—loved the clicking beneath my fingertips.

I wondered. *What if words, sentences, communication could lead to something?* Excitement stirred—if only mildly.

My simple musings proved momentous. Leading me to broader worlds. Toward adventure.

Even romance.

CHAPTER FOURTEEN

KEYBOARDS, COWBOYS and BIG SKY

Accounting. What am I doing in accounting?

My course choice made no sense. Like a Wall Street trader who hadn't seen a live cow striding up to mount an ill-tempered bull at our rodeo.

I had registered at a vocational college locals called Okmulgee Tech, without seeking academic counseling—or common sense. I knew nothing of bookkeeping, had no aptitude for it. Better judgment won out before my second classroom visit ended. The college—later named OSU Institute of Technology—offered many tracks.

The printed word interested me and Teletype included the word 'type'. Working for a newspaper means no shortage of words, nor the name of my new chosen direction — Teletypesetter Perforator Operator.

The high school from which I had recently graduated lacked size and, therefore, course options.

I had wanted very much to gain two skills — Spanish and typing. But administration said I could only choose one. Learn a second language or learn to type—but not both. My plight was bothersome but promptly resolved. I never learned Spanish.

My college instructor now sat at the glorified typewriter and introduced its features. A machine that yielded a stream of punctured tape as the typist pecked the keys. Combinations of the circled holes translated into letters, words and symbols. The coded tape fed into a big linotype machine. Molten lead formed imprints, cooled, took on ink, released the creation to the press room—steps in a process ensuring that paper boys had a product to deliver—the daily or weekly newspaper.

"OK Jerry, give it a try."

Adjusting my chair I rested eight fingertips in their sequence atop familiar symbols. A-S-D-F- . . J-K-L-; (the right pinky paired itself up, as always, with the semi-colon). A good feeling settled in. Eight drifters returning to their common home. In pecking order. Toward the end of my training the department head approached me.

"Jerry, would you consider taking a job far from here?"

The question was my first introduction to the notion that my typing fling may spirit me to sights and places beyond. Both geographical and figurative—to kindred-spirits. To surprises. One of them wrecking me for life, but in a very good kind of way.

My training supervisor studied my face for a response. Obviously knowing something I didn't.

"Yes, I'd be happy to consider it, sir."

"Well, a weekly newspaper called the Cody Enterprise—it's in Wyoming—contacted us. I'm prepared to recommend you for the Operator position if you're interested."

"I would be glad for the opportunity. Yes. Thank you."

So, 20 months removed from an earlier Oklahoma departure, I again boarded a Denver-bound bus—though in a much healthier frame of mind.

A new passenger with a telling weakness for drink stepped aboard in Pueblo, Colorado and sat next to me. Noting the Bible resting open on my lap he slurred an observation.

"Oh! You're readin' the Bible. Good!" His interest rose another level—as did his voice.

"Are you a Christian?" More direct.

"Yes, sir, I am." I was a kid—sure of my faith, but not sure of myself.

"Wonderful! I am too." Then he announced it. "I'm Pentecostal!"

Electing not to fuel the visit by confirming our common faith tradition I offered, "That's nice." He sank contented into his seat and slept. In a moment I glanced his way. *I wonder what's led him to seek comfort, or joy, or escape through a substance in a bottle.* A nudge of compassion stirred. I silently prayed God's care over the random stranger next to me—my fellow Pentecostal.

North of Denver I squinted through a bus window. A passing car sported a red Wyoming license plate. On it I glimpsed a compelling image. A bucking bronco giving his all to dislodge from the saddle an equally determined cowboy. Cheyenne boasted her Frontier Days. Laramie, her Jubilee Days—rodeos taking center stage at each.

Indeed, Wyomingites dubbed themselves the Cowboy State. Stretching myself out, I slid my feet beneath the seat ahead and let my chest pillow my chin. I was soon dreaming of my brother Tim and me. Of Bill, our horse, clippity-clopping under us to Okmulgee's rodeo grounds. To the annual PowWow and Rodeo action.

By the time I stirred, the bus had entered a land of breezy landscapes. The vehicle jostled under wind gusts as it navigated high desert near Casper. Wind River Canyon enthralled us—its rich blue waters snaking along canyon walls. Past Thermopolis the bus climbed to flatter plains, and finally our destination.

Soon we met with a sign along a city street. I chuckled to myself. Why should I be surprised?

Cody, Wyoming—Rodeo Capital of the World.

***

"Excuse me, sir . . . uh, Pardon me."

The raised yet hesitant voice came from the gravel entry into our farm driveway. The dark-skinned gentleman's call turned me to his direction. He was on foot and I looked beyond him to the road. The four-lane highway passing our place linked Tulsa to Dallas and bore the weight of unnumbered vehicles each day.

A long Buick sedan rested on the northbound shoulder, its trunk lid open.

On my Tulsa-to-Cody bus ride my mind revisited that day of a year ago. How did I rally the courage to share my faith with that stranger? And how did I then draw back from another stranger—who asked me of my spiritual life—just hours earlier?

"I'm sorry, sir," the Buick-driver offered, "but would you have a tire jack I could use? I got a flat just now, and my jack is busted."

Drawing a jack from dad's Oldsmobile I joined the visitor. We moved toward his car.

"Where are you headed?" I asked. Eyeing the flat tire, we exchanged general comments—about travel. About weather. As if the elements were listening in, a chilly gust delivered a shiver along my spine.

As we loosed lug nuts and cranked the jack I felt a tug from inside. A sense that I needed to share something of Jesus with the traveler. My pulse picked up as I considered what to say and, as importantly, how to say it. He topped my age by 15 years at least. And he was a man of another race. My mind went to our town's five and dime store of just a few years back. Side-by-side drinking fountains. Twin fixtures—except for labels above them.

"Could I ask you, sir," my turn to respectfully engage. "Umm, do you know Jesus Christ?"

He studied my face a moment—mining its features for sincerity perhaps, or another thing of worth?

Returning to his work, he secured the last lug nut with the tire iron. Gathering my courage, I went on.

"I mean, sir . . . do you know God. In a personal way, as your Savior? Jesus gave his life to save you— make you right with God. He did it for me, too."

The lines of his forehead bunched together. He was thoughtful, not resistant or offended as far as I could tell. My relative calm in the moment surprised me. We deposited the wounded tire into the trunk, shut the lid and dusted our hands. I felt the inner tug again.

"Have you trusted in him? Are your sins forgiven?"

A short pause and his reply.

"No, I haven't, really. Though I know I do need to, you know—need to do it."

"Sir, that's all any of us really need to know. He loves us and just waits for us to turn his way."

"Well," He displayed a stirring. "I think I'm ready to do that turning."

We waited together. A semi-truck roared past, its wind fanning our jackets. Still, the busy highway seemed a distance away.

"Would you be OK kneeling with me here? We can ask God together."

Not waiting, the man knelt to the pavement. I joined him—feeling elated, but tenderly so. Like in a holy place. God's own presence, I thought. Meeting us on Highway 75—Tulsa-bound traffic breezing past.

Our joint prayer was simple. An offering of confession, birthing, of new faith.

"In Jesus' name. Amen."

We stayed kneeling a second longer. The car's bumper—altar of chrome, I thought—served us well. We rose, smiled to each other, embraced. A union of common son-ship conferred by a shared Father. Brothers.

Entering the car, he resumed his journey — with, I thought to myself—an added destination and travelling companion.

My reflections ended.

Lord, up here in the Northwest now, would you bring my heart close? Near to you. Like on that day? Lead me to a family of believers. A church family in Cody—I'd like to feel at home.

A familiar accent lay in store—for just the right time.

***

The bustle and charm of Old-West-revived enveloped Sheridan Avenue. I alighted to my destination's main street in late July, 1964. The summer air was warm—without Oklahoma's thick humidity—indicating the mile-high elevation. Tourism thrived, as it would this time of year.

Resting my suitcase at the curb I stretched. The bus moved on, making Sheridan Avenue's attractions visible across the way.

I shifted my weight to my better leg and took in the flow of tourists streaming in and out of a distinctive lodging marked Irma Hotel. The destination for most lay 50 miles away. I breathed in the mountain air, feeling good about Cody, Wyoming. Eastern Gateway to Yellowstone Park.

Taking up the suitcase I set off for my new quarters four blocks away. Stranger to independent living I settled into a tidy rental room in a private home. No kitchen access.

"Would you like coffee, Sir? I'll take your order when you're ready."

My first morning in Cody found me in a diner two blocks East of The Irma.

I nodded to the young waitress.

"Sure, thanks. And I'll just have a couple eggs over-easy, with bacon and some toast."

The waitress went silent. Her gaze unnerved me. "Uh, Sir. If you don't mind, could you repeat your order?" As I spoke she seemed to dissect each word as it left my mouth.

"Mm, I'm sorry, Sir." She was clearly distracted. And enthused. "Please wait just a moment. I'll be right back!"

In seconds she returned, another waitress near her age in tow.

"Sir? If you don't mind, could I ask you to repeat your order—just once more. For my friend, please?"

Both girls leaned forward. Then I caught on. Neither one knew the Oklahoma drawl—much less spoke it. Even in a tourist town—so far from home— my voice was an oddity. An early morning marvel for a café wait staff.

The matter of accent resurfaced.

After two mornings —on my first Wyoming Sunday—I slipped into Cody's Assembly of God church for worship. In seconds an unmistakable accent seized my attention. I discovered its origin— one of Oklahoma's seventy-seven counties.

Mine.

***

I stood at the entry and surveyed the sanctuary as worshippers trickled in, moved past and made their way to their seats. A gray-haired couple sat ten feet away, near the center aisle to my right. A pianist on the platform up front busied herself with sheet music before taking up a red hymnal.

Hmm, I wonder what songbook the folks do use here. The nearby gray-haired lady held a book of the same reddish tint. My mouth moved as I silently read the title. Cast in gold lettering beneath three delicate crosses it read, Melodies of Praise. I thought. I like that. A song book title with feeling.

Spotting a new visitor the pastor left the platform and came my way. His handshake and generous smile reinforced what I already sensed — the church's warmth. This may be a place I could get to know the Lord better—and some Rocky Mountain dwellers, all at the same time.

"So Jerry, where do you come from? Where would you call home?" The pastor's interest seemed genuine and I warmed to it.

"Well, I come from a small place called Okmulgee. It's in Oklahoma. About 30 miles south of Tulsa."

The mention of Okmulgee struck a chord with the gray-haired lady holding the hymnal. Light refracted on the silver-gray hair as Mom Starr swiveled her head abruptly. Her eyes shimmered and her mouth betrayed delight —through the wrinkled face a little-girl smile. In an accent common to my Oklahoma ears, Mom Starr offered her declaration. She was enthralled.

"Okmulgee?" A brief pause . . . and the clincher. "I went to high school in Preston!"

Astonishment overtook me, even as I smiled at an accent that rendered high school, hah-skoole.

How likely was this? A couple of Okies, she and I. Travelers of a 1200-mile distance to a common place of worship in the Wyoming Rockies. . .Mom Starr and me—united by a common culture—divided by 45 years.

Preston.

Where Typing instructor, Mrs. Schultz acquainted me with circular typing keys. With numbers, letters and symbols mounted on metal stems. I learned in her class to vigorously slide (a thousand times) the feed roller, along the machine at each line's end. Here I entered the world of black carbon paper.

And now, Wyoming. Mrs. Schultz's Typing I and Typing II inaugurated my passage to Wyoming. To Cody. And her warm-hearted people. My vision moved generally toward the church ceiling. *God, could you be doing something?*

Two weeks later found my burgundy suitcase and me at the Starr's front door.

Oklahoma cooking. That will be nice.

***

Known simply as Mom Starr, she took her place behind the lectern. A stickler for faithfulness in Christian duty, she let nothing short of pneumonia deny her its privilege. Hugging a Bible to her chest, she closed her eyes. A more sincere opening prayer I never heard. Her eyes opened and met with those of each person in the small gathering.

"Beloved, let's turn to the Book of Luke. We want to hear some things Jesus said. We'll see him at work and we'll listen to the counsel he gave some villagers. Timely counsel for us today."

It was the Lord's Day. And Mom Starr's adult Sunday School class—homemakers, technicians, newlyweds, oilfield workers—all paid attention.

By my third Sunday in town I counted the Assembly as my church home. Mom and Pop, each of them aging but spry, approached me following worship, that late summer day. Of the pair, Pop was the shorter—maybe by two inches. A sustained twinkle highlighted crows' feet about his eyes, giving the impression that a frown had never visited his face. His trademark chuckle—complete with faint shoulder-tremors—endeared Pop to the community. Mom was slightly stooped, perhaps from compensating over their height discrepancy. She was the more vocal. I was both attracted to and unsettled by a conviction fire that sometimes visited her eyes. I had noticed the odd way her closed lips moved when something important held her thoughts. They moved that way now.

"Jerry, Howard and I would like to give you something to consider."

"Sure."

"We know that where you live doesn't allow for any home-cooked meals. So we were wondering."

Pop Starr nodded.

"Harold and I raised three daughters. They're all grown now and live at their own places. We'd like you to think about moving in with us—try out some of my cooking." Her smile couldn't have been more inviting.

"We can suggest a room-and-board amount and you can decide. Do you think you'd be interested?"

Entering the bedroom with my bit of luggage I took some seconds to adjust my vision. My eyes felt assaulted—by pink.

I'll need no explanation of this. Mom and Pop raised girls all right. The grin at my face broadened as I inventoried my new living quarters.

Bedspread—pink.

Chest-of-drawers—pink.

Curtains and drapes—pink.

Organ music filtered from the living room as I unpacked my suitcase. Afterward I paused at the doorway. My weaker leg wasn't tired. It just felt good to rest against a wall inside a home. Where family dwelled.

The small organ bench supported a contented Pop Starr. Clearly he was at ease in his musician role—and with himself.

Aromas of pot-roast, simmering carrots, potatoes, and who knew what else floated from the modest kitchen. My mouth moistened.

Shortly Mom Starr emerged and sent a smile our way.

"Are you two gents ready to take in some food?"

I entered the kitchen and approached a dining table set for three. And hummed a closing line I was taking in from another room—

"Great is thy faithfulness Lord unto me."

***

"Hi there, Jerry."

I had embarked on my first week at the paper. The eyes of the aproned man twinkled above an authentic smile. "Our new perforator guy, right?" Returning the smile, I nodded.

Buck inspired.

"Mornin' everybody." Again, the gravelly voice of our limping co-worker called from across the shop floor. Curving his arm down and back to secure a shop apron, he flashed the familiar grin—exaggerated as it was to one side.

The term *Jack-of-all-trades* might have originated with him. Often, he was found bent in serious concentration over what the editor deemed newsworthy text in a galley tray. From there he limped back and forth from the king of machines—the towering, rollicking, linotype. Here he pecked out various commands, modifying, as needed some column sent from my keyboard.

Buck's grin sprang to life often in this workplace domain, where odors of ink, fresh or printed paper, molten lead, and oiled shop towels blended. Balancing on and navigating his less-aggravated leg kept him in frequent motion. Lessening discomfort to a hip or knee meant shifting, pivoting, taking one or two short hops when needed. Still, he, remarkably, was not one to murmur.

I wondered how he could do it year after year—at it long before I showed up. His movements about the shop that left me impressed, inspired, convicted.

A grimace gave away his discomfort at times—not intentional nor an invitation to sympathy. It was something people working with him for any time knew. The crusty, resilient, stay-the-distance fellow limped for good cause—one leg was distinctly shorter than the other.

Understanding little of his daily challenges, which far outdistanced my own, I could empathize some. We both limped.

Fiddling with a composing stick in one hand, Buck reached to his favorite mug with the other. "Well, this tray o' type will soon be ready for inking. I'm ready to stop shuffling around this floor. Coffee's what I need." A wry smile formed, highlighting again Buck's slanted mouth-line.

I only later appreciated the quality of his staying power in the face of affliction. Within months I bolted for warmer Oklahoma temperatures, once assailed by arctic-like freezes. Not Buck. He stayed on.

Endearing personalities often emerge through enduring pain.

Most of us can use help in this. Buck's help came—at least in part—through congenial people in the work place.

***

With borrowed carpentry tools I dismantled the wooden crate my dad shipped from Oklahoma. Soon I straddled the unpacked merchandise and thrust the kick-starter. I was happy for the right-foot design. With my left foot's polio history firing up the motorcycle engine would have been tough.

The 150cc Honda came to me a couple days after my bus arrival on Sheridan Avenue. Sitting on my bike felt good—a link with my home state, and memories. A wistful mood took me back.

I was ecstatic over my bike's achievement one night. On the Honda I had opened the throttle on a long downhill stretch of highway, seeing what she could do.

Returning to the town's main street, I spotted a familiar green and white '59 Chevrolet—the wheelsof a good friend. The Chevy was parked before a diner. Dropping the bike's kickstand I strode in, primed to brag. At a booth I spotted my brother, Tim, his friend Larry and a couple of others.

"Guys! Guess what. I just got 70 on my Honda!"

Gale, the Chevy owner and the wittiest among us, grinned my direction. "Kinda crowded wasn't it?"

Another memory was the goose egg my skull acquired from a Sixth Street pavement. I smiled again at the remark, "Reckon we oughta get his bike off the road?"

Now my same white Honda carried me along the Shoshone River, into and past a canyon. The smell of Shoshone's sulphur pestered my nostrils as I leaned into highway curves. The bike hummed loudly through tunnels leading to the Buffalo Bill Reservoir. Cloud shadows blotched Rattlesnake and Cedar Mountains. Peaks that—like sentries—stood watch over Cody. I ventured between them, then past the lake and up Wapiti Valley.

My motorcycle treks became therapy rides—
the perfect answer to hours parked in a chair near an
editor's room, where my fingers marathon-danced on
teletype keys.

Weather attractive to motorcyclists held on
until early fall. Tourism slowed. Intermittent cold
snaps knocked at Cody's door, ready to usher in an
approaching winter.

For the Honda and me, a last big trek lay
ahead—toward the most unexpected, life-altering
adventure.

***

At 60 miles per hour, cold pummeled my face.
The mountain air continued its assault as Cody,
Wyoming, receded back of me to the south. I had left
before 7 a.m. My destination this Labor Day Sunday
was Billings, Montana. To lessen my discomfort I
dialed the throttle back a notch with my right hand. I
was shivering.

This was ranch land in the raw. Clusters of
sheep—like huddling athletes in white jerseys—
congregated near one another, though not as tightly
as in serious weather. My bike took me past similar

groupings of cattle in the open range. An occasional head rose among them, nostrils emitting puffs of steam.I crossed the state line. Minutes into Big Sky Country I slowed. Surveying the quiet main street of small-town Belfry I hoped for an open diner with hot food. *I must dismount this bike and catch a break. I'm freezing!*

Ah. Seems like a cozy cafe. Indeed, and at my journeys' halfway point—a refuge. I requested my standard—two eggs over-easy, bacon, toast, and black coffee. I smacked my gloved palms together and circled in short steps before a wood-burning stove. Beyond the effects of frigid conditions common to most people, my earlier polio encounters seemed to have marginally stifled my circulation. Despite my attempts to thaw my fingers, another two minutes passed once my order came before I held a fork with any ease. My thoughts reached for images I hoped lay ahead.

It'll be nice seeing Brother Fred and his family. I anticipated Montana's largest city as I spread strawberry jam on my toast.

Fred. The third man of the Creason brothers intersecting my world. I suppose I should have let them know I would come see them today.

The waitress extended a navy blue coffee pot—steam levitating above its spout. "More coffee?" I nodded gratefully.

Fred Creason, his kind German wife, Erica, and their two young boys had, until recently, lived in my hometown, Okmulgee. Members of our church family. Fred, in the insurance business, moved his family to Billings on what some would call a whim. A mystery dream, believed by Fred to have been God-sent, played a role.

A thought interrupted my reflections, tightening my eyebrows.

Never one to fuss very much over planning ahead, I realized now I lacked some important information. Quite important.

I had no Billings address for the Creason family. Nor a Creason telephone number. Further, I only assumed they knew that I now resided in Cody—100 miles near.

Wow. They could be off someplace on vacation for all I know. And, the Creasons are my only reason for visiting Billings. I don't know another soul in all Montana. Well—something will work out, I guess. I had never seriously pondered the word, naïve.

Stretching, I pushed back from the breakfast table and reviewed my road map. Then I took up my wool coat, thick scarf and rabbit-hair gloves. I glanced at a wall clock. It was just past 8:00 a.m. when I stepped from the diner.

My first breakfast in Montana. Nice, I mused, cinching my helmet strap. I eyed the northward highway and wondered about the town called Billings. And the Creason family's whereabouts.

Something lay before me I could have never foreseen. Within hours I would meet someone. From this another journey would spring. A larger, life-impacting one.

Of callings. Of dreams. Of covenant.

CHAPTER FIFTEEN

MONTANA GIRL

The term reasonable and prudent measured Montana's legal highway speed for years. Absent a daytime speed limit, drivers simply focused on the road ahead, rather than fixating on radar-fitted patrol cars or their own speedometers. Some motorists argue that Big Sky highways were safer in those earlier times—when reasonable and prudent described people themselves—not just speed laws. My small-engine motorcycle threatened neither Montana nor Wyoming law enforcement of the '60s.

As I crossed railway tracks at the south edge of Laurel, Montana, I was within 20 miles of my destination. It's funny how our senses usher us to times and locations. And memories. With its oil refinery, Laurel's sights and smells wakened feelings of another place. From the highway entering Tulsa we saw refineries layer the atmosphere in smoke plumes, spreading their billows adrift like a giant bedcovering flung from a housekeeper's invisible hands. Near the highway white storage tanks shadowed a larger-than-life sign boldly declaring, Tulsa, Oklahoma—Oil Capital of the World.

Well, it's Sunday morning in Montana. If the Creason family is around, in a few minutes they're likely entering a church. Somewhere.

Downtown Billings was quiet. The abrasive air began to mellow as the sun made its upward climb. Leaving the parked Honda, I entered an upscale hotel and surveyed the lobby. There were two mahogany phone booths, side by side—neither of them occupied. It wasn't a telephone I sought. I flipped through the directory to the Yellow Pages.

C-h-u—there it was. Churches. Hmm. Even for a city of 60,000 this seemed a lot of churches.

Let's see... Non-denominational. If the Creasons are not away, they're probably, maybe. Beneath the category the tip of my forefinger glided downward. Plenty of listings here, too.

A ballpoint pen, attached to a thin chain, lay close at hand. Resting my finger at a random name I copied the church and its address. It didn't occur to me to copy any of the others.

Without the aid of a city map I directed my bike down a side street just beyond the hotel. After two or three turns, within a few blocks I was at the street I sought. Minutes after leaving the phone booth I spotted the church sign, Tabernacle of Faith. I tipped the open end of my left glove. My watch read 9:45.

An outer church stairway led me up to the entrance. The warmth of the sanctuary enveloped me and I paused to take in the room and scan the few early arrivals. Drawing a long breath I smiled broadly.

Erica Creason—Fred's war bride (as the era designated her)—spotted me. Her German accent traversed the sanctuary. "Fred! Boys."

Erica remained astonished. Her eyes glistened. "Look. It is Jerry Lout!"

The foursome descended on me. Exclamations punctuated our laughter as we hugged.

Pretty amazing, I thought. *The first place to look. And here they are. The Creasons. Wow.*

Our mini-reunion quieted as piano music signaled an opening hymn. Taking up a red song book I fingered the graphic. Three gilded crosses. The corners of my mouth turned upward. *Melodies of Praise.* Throughout worship I felt closeness. Close to friends, close to others in the room —even the strangers. I felt close in our common purpose to gather in this place—to worship the Lord, to grow in our faith. What church is about, I thought. Following the morning sermon, the Creasons brought me to the preacher.

"Brother Barnes, we want to introduce you to Jerry Lout. He's a friend from Oklahoma, from our church body there."

Pastor Earl Barnes, a gregarious man, smiled. He welcomed me, then signaled his family. I recognized the approaching woman as the organist. She carried herself with grace. Her smile was full, sincere.

"Jerry, this is my wife, Mary, and our three children."

I nodded. He indicated their two boys. "Our sons here are Jonathan and David. And this is their sister."

The pretty 15-year-old stood relaxed but poised. She held a scarf and woolen cap. Across an arm draped a winter coat that would soon conceal the light blue sweater she wore. Her name was Alice. Her blond hair framed a face as attractive as any I had ever seen and I risked an extra second to study it. Her eyes especially drew me. I forced myself to shift my gaze from their symmetry and beauty. I turned to acknowledge again her mother and father.

The girl's first name was Alice. But she went by her middle name.

Ann.

***

Reuniting with Creasons made for a happy Labor Day. The northwest air mellowed over the weekend and was kind on my return cycle trip home, to Cody.

Winter swept in. I really liked my Honda. Logic won out. In a nostalgic mood I traded it for a cozier ride—a car I could wish were mine today. The make was Chevrolet; the model, 1957.

With winter came bitter cold. The coldest day of my working life found me stuffing newspapers into the night for the weekly distribution.

Equipment had ceased running and it was everyone on deck. A main gas line erupted outside town, shutting energy off to the city. By candlelight our Cody Enterprise crew stuffed papers until midnight.

Mom and Pop Starr's home felt arctic when I finally crept in. Taking a banana from the kitchen counter, I found it solid. Peeling it I bit in. At current room temperature its coldness rivaled a banana split. That night I went to bed fully clothed. Only my shoes remained uncovered. We learned next morning of the 35 below zero temperature that night. By a miracle no lives were lost among the elderly or ill and the gas line returned to service.

I spent my leisure times with the church youth near my age. Richard and Rommie became sweet on two sisters—Judy and Joyce. The quartet received me into their circle as if Wyoming were my native home, and as if five weren't an uneven number. I was happy in this fun, caring community. Our short jaunts carried with them sounds of current pop music. Strains of "In The Misty Moonlight" from the car's open window—our harmonies mellowing the night air. Romantic music carries power. In time wedding bells rang for the two couples.

For a while I dated a nice town girl. We each discerned the difference between friendship and courtship early on. Our dating trailed off with no hurt feelings.

In time I found myself missing the Fred Creason family. I had been sure to get their phone contact, and I dialed the Billings number. Yes, they were in next weekend and would welcome a visit. Fred added that after Sunday worship they would join the Barnes family for dinner. Fred assured me I would be welcome as their guest.

My heart picked up its beat. A visit to the pastor's home. I would see the pretty girl with the pretty eyes who went by her middle name. Ann.

It was nice the Creasons hadn't moved away.

***

Waving off an annoying bumblebee, I imagined Cody, Wyoming.

Her sunny sky, crisp, late June air. A far cry from 90 degree temps and 90percent humidity baking me now, I inwardly moaned, not to mention the bee. I gripped my straw hat and swung. The hat connected, the pest darting off in a zigzag exit.

Since I had abruptly bailed on my employer during Christmas season, my return to Oklahoma yielded nothing in decent job prospects. The nearest was a brief stint scouting and reporting on local happenings for a weekly newspaper. The Freelance was 16 miles south of my parent's place where I was again living. For now. Except for the pay, I liked the work. A token bonus from writing was the occasional ego lift.

Though I had a weakness for puns I earned a *by Jerry Lout* byline on a piece now and then.

Firemen responded one night to a floor furnace incident. Involved were a pair of neglected rubber boots and a lot of smoke.

"Soles Rescued from Flames" drew smiles around the copy editor's desk. But clever text didn't translate into better pay. I left the job—giving notice this time—when I saw my earnings hardly covered fuel for the work commute. And, there was the accident. Going home one afternoon just before I gave my notice, my Chevy's rear panel was crumpled by a driver failing to yield at a red light. At Sixth and Wood Drive—not far from my motorbike mishap of an earlier time.

Since leaving the reporter job I had kept applying for work. Newspapers, print shops, any place I might hone skills where ink and paper converge; to become once more—as the term goes— gainfully employed.

Cattle and farming work, if done well, demands diligent attention.

To aid my dad I had hooked up the rotary mower to a Farmall. Jostling over pastureland, I set out for the mission. Trim 20 acres of unwanted sapling sprouts and other undergrowth threatening to sabotage haying season.

My dad's tractor and I looped the 20-plus acres. Each round reduced the distance by the mower's width.

Mowing pastureland . . . is this my destiny?

A snake, hardly visible in the Bermuda ahead, scurried from the machine's path.

With half the pasture yet to mow, I pressed the clutch fully in. The tractor and rig halted.

It was time I visited a minute with God.

I had come to him a lot over past months. Conversing with him about employment and, in the end, feeling lifted. My problem—the lifted feeling didn't stay long. What followed became short cycles—an added prayer visit, another wait, discouragement, impatience. Another specially added prayer time. And so on.

I cut the ignition. The exhaust gave a sharp belch and went quiet.

I had grown to detect melancholy when it drifted my way. It hung about me now. I tilted my head back, took in the sky and—dreary mood aside— yielded up a resolve. It came verbally—unrehearsed and not even thought of 30 seconds earlier. The resolve needed voicing. Now. Not with bluster, but deliberate, still.

"Father. I belong to you. I've applied all over for work with no result. Lord, here and now I tell you that I'm yours. Regardless. If you give me a job today or if you don't for ten thousand years, I'm yours." I paused before concluding. "I give it to you."

Whenever praying it was always to God. And his son in mind. *Thank you, Jesus. Thank you, God.*

A lightness settled in. Unusual. Tangible. Even carefree.

I touched the ignition. The motor coughed once, then settled into its rhythmic drone. I looked at the dusty face of my wristwatch. About time for lunch.

A few minutes passed and I was at our home's back door slapping hay fragments from my blue jeans. I entered and heard mom call, "Your sandwich is about ready, dearie." Mothers and their expressions!

"Oh, Jerry, do you know a Mr. Newman? He called a few minutes ago; wants you to call him back. A Muskogee number."

Newman. . . Muskogee. My eyebrow lifted.

"Well—yeah. I applied a while back at a Muskogee paper, the Phoenix."

The shop supervisor answered my dial.

"Hello, Mr. Newman. This is Jerry Lout."

"Are you still interested in working for our newspaper, Mr. Lout?"

"Yes, sir."

"When could you begin? Can you come in Monday?"

Setting the phone back I stared at it a minute. And wagged my head. *Mowing on Friday. Typesetting on Monday.* The thought that followed produced a chuckle at first. A sense of wonder next.

I'm a fella with a job. In under 10,000 years.

"When I pray coincidences happen, and when I don't, they don't"   - William Temple

***

Driving my little blue Pontiac near San Antonio's 410 Loop in 1969 I dialed the car radio and caught the rhythms of a new country release. My thoughts drifted back four years to the image of a nondescript city limits sign, one I had often passed en route to work. It bore the name of an Indian people, the Muscogee.

The Muskogee job, opening after my Bermuda-field prayer session, set me on a new course. Simply recalling my mom's statement—"Mr. Newman wants you to call"—stirred feelings.

Landing the job, I did the daily, 80-mile roundtrip commute from the Okmulgee farm. One night returning home my car hit an icy patch on a long curve. Whoa, careful now, Chevy. Swinging the steering wheel right, then left—tapping the brake pedal, I rode the spinning car to an eventual, safe halt. A life-long conviction took root that night about winter driving. Snow-covered Wyoming roads are generally little match—danger-wise—to Oklahoma's all-too-common black ice. I moved to Muskogee.

I grew to admire my engineering friend, Larry, who lived in the rooming house I moved to—especially his attention to physical wellness. I carry in my head a scene of Larry ingesting a small mountain of vitamin tablets and capsules every morning—long before fitness became faddish.

I moved to Tulsa after a time, working for an aircraft manufacturer. The job worked well.

***

I wonder if she'll write back. Shoot, I thought, *I wonder if she'll even remember me.*

When the first-ever Montana-postmarked letter came my way I hadn't prepared for the warm feeling that struck me, drawing me straight into her greeting. Over months—then years—her response letters came—all affecting me the same way. Warmly.

Recalling an old movie scene, I glanced self-consciously around, brought the letter near and sniffed.

Well, whether perfume's on or not, it sure feels like it smells nice.

I suspected romance was at my door when, once or twice I purposefully held off opening a letter from Ann. Arriving home from work I spotted a Billings letter my landlady had dropped at my door. Like an adolescent I took it in hand, willing myself to not open it—just to see how long I could delay. The wait may have lasted two minutes.

Though the handwritten dispatches from the pretty Billings girl likely didn't fit the romantic letter category, they found me often humming a pop hit of the times. *L-O-V-E.*

News filtered down of a coming layoff at the Douglas aircraft plant.

"I've got a little savings," I muttered, opening a drawer in search of my old U.S. road map.

The line my forefinger traced led westward out of Tulsa—then north.

CHAPTER SIXTEEN

FINE PRINT

It was springtime—a Saturday—when I entered the Pancake House. She had waitressed here since entering high school.

Despite our two-and-a-half years of letter writing, I felt shy in her presence. Finding a stool at the counter, I waited while my lovely (undeclared) girlfriend, in her blue print dress and restaurant apron, finished up with a customer.

Spotting me she paused. We exchanged smiles—between lingering and fleeting. She saw to another customer then came my way.

"Hi."

Ann greeted me and, not wishing to assume I lacked interest in the restaurant menu, added, "Would you like something?"

"Sure, thanks. Just coffee. Uh, black."

She brought my drink. New customers entered.

Not the time to catch up on news, I thought.

I finished my ten-cent cup of coffee. A quarter found its way next to the dime. Her tip.

Through an earlier phone visit we had arranged a drive to Cody for the following day. An inconspicuous wave and I was gone.

Sunday morning we stepped from her front door to my Chevy. I opened the passenger door. As she entered the car I caught the scent of her perfume.

I turned the car's ignition and looked at my watch. Seven-thirty.

Facing Ann I smiled, "Can't wait for Mom and Pop Starr to meet you."

Though I lacked any real plan, my outing—on this day, with this girl—exceeded all I might have hoped for.

The Cody pastor and his wife—along with Mom and Pop Starr, acquaintances, friends— everyone welcomed. Wide smiles. Spirited chatting.

Pastor Siggins asked me to share at the evening service. Our return trip to Billings would set the course for something special. After the evening meeting we waved goodbye. I turned the Chevy toward Montana.

Crossing the state line we travelled a distance in silence, arriving at a place where roads converge—a mile south of Bridger, Montana. Slowing the car, I eased to the stop sign where Highways 72 and 310 cross.

A fine place for a kiss maybe, I thought.

It was our first.

The miles and minutes between the kiss and her town—between Bridger and Billings—swept by barely noticed.

How will I ask her? Is tonight the best time to ask her? Take a breath. Think. I cared little for thinking. *What if we could just be here, like this, forever?*

I sent a glance to the lighted instrument panel past the steering wheel. My heart skipped a beat and a trace of moisture surfaced on my palms. *Oh boy.*

One—two—three miles. They crawled by, while my vision darted back and forth between the panel gauge and an unlit horizon out ahead. The landscape yielded an occasional pinprick of light—ranch houses far off the highway, flanking our path.

I really liked Montana. Her wildness, her grand, expansive spaces. But now... I willed my mind to screen out unkind depictions of Big Sky Country. Terms like secluded, deserted, forsaken. Even Primitive. *Gee,* I thought, *even Oklahoma has a gas station every now and then.* Unfair comparisons, I knew. They were efforts to excuse myself for my own negligence. *Well. I might want to think about that tomorrow. Oh boy.*

Finally we entered a town. It slumbered peacefully.

For one whose sleep just got interrupted, the gas station man displayed patience. Meeting the need, sending us on our way.

"Well, we're about there." The lights of Ann's city reflected off the night sky not far ahead.

Once in town I steered the car to a wide shoulder off the street. Edging the vehicle forward, I brought it to a stop beneath a street lamp. I faced her. In a voice I hoped sounded natural, I asked, "OK if we have a few minutes before getting you to your place?"

The prettiest girl I had ever known nodded. A slight turn and she directly faced me. Those eyes. *Golly, to look into them every day. What would that be like?*

We talked a little, revisiting events of the day in Cody, punctuating comments with light laughter. Then came a pause. I cleared my throat.

"Um, Ann, I want to say," my voice had taken a serious tone, yet I found the words coming with surprising ease. Not rushed but steady, quiet, direct.

"I care a lot for you, Ann. I love you. I want to ask you to marry me." She was quiet, sensing there was something else.

"But I also need to tell you", I breathed once then continued, "I feel God has called me to serve him as a missionary. In Africa."

To think that I had actually voiced this, had appealed to this wonderful girl to say yes to my proposal. And notifying her, in the same breath, I would take her far from home if she answered, yes. And not just her Montana-home—her America-home.

The street-lamp lighted the car interior, bringing her face and so, any expressions, into easy view. She smiled and the smile was natural and warm. Her response to my proposal was silence. At first.

She then began recounting a single incident from an earlier time.

"When I was little", she began, "around nine years old—a visiting pastor spoke at our church. He had been in Asia."

Wherever this story might lead, it clearly carried weight with her.

"I was moved by the man's message. He told of lost people, locked away. Like in prisons, but not physical prisons. In spiritual prisons with nobody to show them a way out."

I followed Ann's words. A warmth was there. The girl I had come to love—barely eighteen— beautiful eyes viewing me from her beautiful face. She continued.

"After the service, when we went home I said to my parents that I had something to tell them.

"'Dad, Mom,' I said, 'When I grow up I am going to be a missionary. To Africa.'"

Ann smiled my way, offering a soft chuckle as I sat astonished, unbelieving. She went on, "My dad said, 'No Ann. There are snakes in Africa, and you hate snakes.'

"I love you too, Jerry."

I was quiet a moment, savoring those last words—then asked a single-sentence question—wanting to confirm what I hoped I was hearing.

Her smile widened further, "Yes—enough to marry you."

***

Was this a bad idea?

The optic breakthrough overtaking the nation met me in Davenport. I gave the plastic inserts a try when a bargain price pulled me. But blinking ensued and wouldn't let up. Contact lenses might not be for me.

My dad had taken a plumbing job there. He and mom would have several months more in Davenport. "Welcome traveler," they had chimed in on my arrival from Montana.

After my eventful visit to Ann I had routed my return back home through the state of Iowa. Three things occurred in my few days' stop-over. First my attempt at employment. "Sorry. I'm afraid we don't have a teletype-setter position opening right now."

Well, anyway I consoled myself, I gave it my best try to get on with the Times-Democrat.

My second Iowa action was tossing my conventional eye-glasses. Since age 12 I had worn them. Bad idea. Fashioned of harsh, inflexible material, the lenses pestered me from the start. My staccato blinking did not let up. I would give up on contacts within a year.

Thirdly, I made a phone call back to Billings—to a clergyman. Not just any clergyman. It embarrassed me that, in my haste to ask Ann to be my wife, I had leapfrogged protocol. .

"Hello, Brother Barnes . . . Mm, I would like to ask . . . "

Ann's father was kind—approving my marriage proposal and his daughter's yes—now that he knew of it.

Thanking him, I brought the visit to a close, returned the phone to its hook, and exhaled long and slow.

"Your cooking's as good as ever, Mom." Suitcase in hand, I touched the doorknob of their rented mobile home.

I had better get back to Oklahoma.

A guy who's getting married had best get a job.

***

My index finger touched the rotary disc. I dialed the figures scrawled on the paper before me. A job lead, maybe?

The seconds taking me to dial had me reflecting, *Boy oh boy, just yesterday it seems.*

I was five years old—shedding the leg brace. Then nine—hospitalized by the second polio bout.

My thoughts easily moved to the dear angel on crutches. *What an impact she had made. still does,* I mused.

The voice in the phone receiver brought me back.

"Hello, this is Richard."

Placing Richard's voice was easy. Ultra-deep bass. Warm, of a kind surely passed to him from an older sister. Opaline.

"Hi, Richard. This is Jerry returning your call. How are things?"

A short exchange then, "Jerry I'm calling to let you know the aerospace company I'm with is hiring. If you'd be interested in a Tulsa job, I think you might get on."

My first day saw me trudging through rows of filing shelves—aisle upon aisle of engineering data. I thought of my earlier years when I had peered at oddly-textured, blue-tinted paper spread across the hood of my father's pickup. His fingers traced images while his mind tracked their silent messages. Here, taking in rows of files, my senses mingled. Feeling the green, metal pickup hood beneath my palms, smelling the print-room chemicals from the nearby room in this place. Wow, I never imagined so many blueprints.

The company, its employees in the thousands, processed me for security clearance. Heady stuff for a country boy raised on an acreage south of there.

The United States' and Soviet Union's race for space had launched in earnest. Brilliant American minds developed and crafted a top priority project.

Where will all this lead? I wondered. Over coming months my hands probed after, retrieved, refiled blueprints by the hundreds

Many bore a name out of Greek mythology.

Apollo.

***

Where is that box?

Silently pressing the question upon myself, I discreetly probed the floorboard under my driver's seat. A couple seconds went by. Ah!

Drawing out the jewelry box, I muted a whistle of relief and shielded the box from view. *That could have been close,* I worried. *How dumb—leaving it out here in the car to begin with.*

***

Hours earlier Ann's flight from Salt Lake City had begun its approach. Hungry for a first glimpse, I studied the northwestward sky beyond Tulsa's airport.

In minutes the plane taxied to a halt. A door opened. Heavy August air, the likes of which she had never breathed, overtook my fiancée. It carried with it a flavor. Pungent. Strong. Oil-like. From her platform vantage point she glanced the landscape before her. A refinery must be on the airfield, she guessed. Years afterward, mention of Tulsa evoked in her a 1967 memory. A refinery-flavored Oklahoma summer day.

"Hi Ann. Hi! I'm here!"

She spotted me. We laughed and quickly moved to each other.

"Here, I'll take that."

Minutes later I rested her luggage by the car. Retrieving keys from a pocket, I opened the low-hanging passenger door of my blue Karmann Ghia. Before she stooped to enter, we embraced. "Welcome to Tulsa."

I turned the ignition. "You've got to be hungry! There's a neat restaurant near downtown."

"Oh?" she asked, "What's it called?" I paused. "Jerry's." We laughed again.

"We'll grab a bite there, then head for the movie. I've heard it's pretty good."

***

"The hills are alive . . ."

The actress's sunny voice, her free and happy dance set in the beauty of Austria's Alps—all swept us up in the big screen's magic.

Tulsa's Brook Theater had premiered the musical two years earlier. A smash hit, it drew movie goers to the site in a continuous run for more than a year. Here it was—back again now. Neither of us had seen it before. What perfect timing, I thought.

My arm lay atop the theater seat behind her. Ann rested her head there. Under my breath and to the musical sound I mimed a lyric of my own. *My heart is alive —with the sound of. . .* And thought of a special item—secure I hoped—beneath a car seat outside the theater. Our common love of music had us each humming the melodies before reaching the exit doors.

We sunk into our respective bucket seats of the Ghia. With my left hand I reached beneath mine and retrieved a small square box. Opening it, I announced with all the valor I could muster,

"And this, Miss Ann Barnes, is yours." I slipped the diamond on her finger. "Thank you for saying 'yes.'" Lucky me. The ring fit.

"Mom. Dad. You came!"

My parent's arrival to Oklahoma caught us by surprise. Their impromptu trip from Iowa during Ann's week-long visit ensured that they met my future bride well ahead of our December wedding.

For the remaining days left after our evening at the movies we rationed every chance to be together. Most such times went great. One or two others, not so much.

"Ann, let me show you a pretty little spot near the country club." I figured our drag-Main-and-Wood-Drive evening could do with a change so I steered the car down a narrow gravel road. A small body of water came into view.

"What do you think of our Kitty Lake?"

The Karmann Ghia had rolled to a quiet stop before the pond. Moonlight glittered on miniature waves separating us from a tree-strewn shore not far beyond. Crickets, frogs and locusts serenaded us a good 40 minutes. Time to move along, I tried the ignition. Then once more. And again.

Aw, crazy car, start, will ya! The words were silent, uttered in frustration within my head.

I kept my cool enough but nothing I did coaxed the VW to life. "I'm sorry, Ann. This thing bugs me like this every now and then." More futile attempts.

"Uh, again I'm really sorry. Mm, would you mind taking the wheel while I push? If the speed gets up enough you know how to pop the clutch, right?"

"Uh-huh."

If I felt like a dingbat now, the night was young.

The car's out-of-date console had issues. Sliding from passenger to driver seat Ann felt a catch and heard a noise no owner of a new garment welcomes. The dress ripped on a metal shard. The new dress.

I pushed the car with all I had, my lovely fiancée at the wheel trying to do her part. The engine refused to fire. Exasperated, I rallied a homeowner who let me make a call.

"Uh, Hi sis.

"Mm, I have a problem."

My mechanically gifted brother-in-law got us moving again after another forty minutes.

Sparkling Kitty Lake receded back of us as the car climbed from the valley. I soon dropped my special date at Betty's home, her Oklahoma lodging for now. Trudging back to my car, recalling Ann's ripped new dress, I heaped contempt on my unreliable wheels, and then on myself,

Dingbat.

Next day the mood was lighter. Still, I vowed we'd find a different vehicle once the wedding came and once we could swing the cost.

***

"Well, I really don't like this."

The day of Ann's flight to Billings after her week-long Oklahoma visit was much like the day of her arrival those days before. Same airport road. Same Southern Plains climate. A lot of same. The not same was my mood. Seven grand days were ending. I would soon stand on the wrong side of an airplane door.

She looked up at me. "We'll be back together soon, Jerry." I loved her voice, her Rocky Mountain accent. She was right, of course. It wouldn't be long. I so looked forward to passing my years in the company of this woman.

I had hardly stopped turning her way throughout our week together—taking in her soft beauty. Such eyes. Without effort on her part, her look drew me toward her as strongly as at our first meeting three years ago. I looked now. The strength of her mind, too. *This is one bright girl,* I mused. A mild twinge of guilt stirred. Marrying me meant forfeiting a full academic ride she was assured of at a Montana college. I did not permit the guilty feeling to advance beyond mild.

"OK, it won't be so long. If you say so."

We kissed, and held one another a moment. She moved to the plane's door. Once the plane was airborne, I stared at the sky until a cloud finally swallowed the tiny dot.

***

VOWS

On a November day in 1967 a silver-haired Okmulgee businessman picked up his phone and dialed. The lady on the receiving end had booking confirmations in hand.

"Thank you for calling, sir. Yes, your booking is confirmed, the lodging will be ready. A double for two overnights in one of our cozy Lake Wister cabins. . . Yes, that is correct", she verified, "the nights of December 30th and 31st."From his office, the gentleman voiced a crisp reminder before hanging up. "Be sure to charge this to my account."

"Thank you, we certainly will, sir."

***

"Sure glad we didn't hit any bad winter storm coming down here."

Ann's father was cheery. He and his family, including the bride, had made the late December drive a few days ahead of the wedding.

The countdown was on. One afternoon, my parents stood with Ann and me at our family residence. Dad was clearly pleased, smiling as he nodded in the direction of the dwelling before us, "Yes, three months, a little gift from your mother and me."

I voiced our gratitude, my fiancée at my side beaming, "Wow, the first whole three months—rent-free? Wow. Thanks Mom and Dad!"

I lingered in the farm driveway and surveyed the two-story home. My parents had moved out of it after us kids were grown and gone. Ann and I would begin our married life here. Dad had renovated the old family dwelling, turning it into a trio of rental apartments.

I looked to the single upper story window and wondered how many early mornings had my feet left the toasty warmth of blankets to land on that cold linoleum floor? The memory was vivid. I'd dash across to the little white space heater, its low flames emitting enough warmth to draw me quickly to it. My mind called up the little dance ritual I repeated every winter morning—hopping with my right foot, the better one. Then to the limping one—exercising more creativity now to stay upright. The dance ended once my limbs found their home inside my cold Wrangler jeans.

Imagine, I thought as my mind returned to the present, *I'll soon be a married man, living with a wife under this same roof that I've known so long. It will be our home. At least for a while.*

***

Earl J. Barnes, father of the bride, presided over our wedding. The ceremony fit well with the times in Oklahoma's small town culture. Tasteful, few frills. Attractive. Traditional.

Before our wedding day, Ann's father had voiced his counsel to the two of us with a pair of conspicuous statements,

"When I tie the knot it's tied. . . Keep out of debt."

The pianist struck a strong note and the guests rose. The Wedding March began.

How lucky can a fella be? Ann's white-gowned image at the chapel's entryway held me, leaving me feeling in the moment that only the two of us occupied the sanctuary. I felt elated and undeserving all at once—country bumpkin to nobility.

She had taken her escort's arm. A long time ago this silver-haired gent, teaching youngsters in vacation Bible school, coins jingling in a trouser pocket, handed me a terrific gift, a "doorway" to experience more of Jesus. Remarkably, he had later on met Pastor Earl Barnes when visiting Montana. Their friendship grew. Now Brother Madison moved down the aisle—presenting to me in her father's stead, another gift—a precious gift, indeed. My bride.

"Do you, Ann Barnes, take this man to be your wedded husband. . ."

At the exchanging of rings, my brother moved to a place near the piano. Tim's strong baritone brought out the very best in the love song. *More.*

***

A few minutes down the road, I turned to Ann, "Mrs. Jerry Lout, I don't know about you, but my grinning muscles are frozen in place. I've never smiled so much and for so long in my life."

Back in the Reception Hall we had—in keeping with tradition, unwrapped every individual wedding gift—smiling our thanks the whole time. Well-wishers joked and laughed around the cake and punch table.

A light rain was falling when I opened the Volkswagen's passenger door. My new bride laughed at the long shreds of rain-drenched toilet paper clinging to the hood and rooftop. Tin cans rattled behind us as we pulled away from jubilant, waving friends. Our destination was a quaint, romantic spot two hours south. Lake Wister. Still another gift to us.

From Brother Madison.

***

Our lives together had begun.

"Honey, look at this." Weeks after our December 30, 1967 wedding, I turned to Ann's laughing voice. Her open palm revealed several grains of rice.

"Let me guess. . . the Volkswagen floorboard from wedding night? It's a lost cause, baby, we'll never clear it all out." Three months into married life we met our first hurdle—a crisis of health. Standing at our apartment's living room entrance, Ann clutched her chest. Her eyes widened in pain as she struggled, taking in short gasps of air. The ER trip confirmed her guess—and introduced to me a new medical term: TE Fistula. A doctor scheduled an esophageal dilation—a measure taken to stretch the esophagus allowing food to more easily reach her stomach. Years had passed since Ann's last episode and treatment. A crisis at the time of her birth had started the problem.

***

— March, 1949 —

"Nurse. Nurse! Please. My baby's choking on her milk!" Mary Barnes' eyes filled with fear. This was not the first signal of something unusual. Since her baby's birth, the baby failed to properly take in liquids. "Please, something is really wrong." Hours passed. "Mr. and Mrs. Barnes, when a preborn baby is developing, a rare malformation can happen." Ann's parents went silent as the surgeon explained. "Normally, the esophagus (taking food to the stomach) and the trachea (taking air to the lungs), don't connect with one another. If they do, something called a TE Fistula (tracheoesophageal fistula) occurs. Without urgent surgery, babies have drowned. Others have lost their lives to pneumonia." By the time of Ann's birth. Few operations of this nature had proved successful. Sobered by this knowledge, the surgeon was direct. Touching Mary Barnes' hand he spoke to each of them. "We will do our best."

God. Please. Help my daughter. Earl Barnes made the appeal silently. He had entered into an experience in God's presence at one point during his service with the U.S. Navy. Lacking helpful guidance afterward, his spiritual life had drifted.

With a radical incision through the infant's back and another, a frontal approach near the abdomen, the operation was underway. Hours later the doctor's update brought tears of relief to the young parents, "We will watch closely in the coming days. I believe it worked." The physician, thankfully, was right. Left over, however, from the complex surgery, were complicating issues—scar tissue, a still-narrow food passageway among them. Courageously, my young bride endured the esophageal stretching procedure—an exercise to be repeated later on. Moving with Ann past the clinic door and onto the parking lot, I remembered a wall plaque I had once seen, Life is fragile, *handle with prayer.*

***

A few months later my own medical crisis erupted. It was the day I gained a new perspective about pain meds.

"Really honey—no pain pills?" Ann asked. "You didn't bring any home?"

"I winced. "It didn't hurt that much after the first aid people sewed up my hand . . . so I told them I wouldn't need any." The memories of that afternoon on the job were all too vivid.

Bounding over hardware, Francis had reached me in three strides. Seizing my wrist, he had squeezed evenly. The blood flow, shooting spurts of red a moment earlier, eased. "Here Jerry, do this. I'll shut the machine down." I took over my co-worker's self-assigned medic role, clasping my right wrist. Francis, the worker, returned in seconds. "Now, we want to get you to First Aid." Reproductions department had moved me to their shop in the massive aeronautics plant. The square, open room, seasoned with inky aromas, pulsed with print machine rhythms. I had come to draw odd comfort from the omnipresent, clickity-clack movements of the press room. I had wrapped up the final job order on my multilith press for the day, clearing away some stragglers of unspent paper. Standing before the unit, I dialed down the ink roller speed, then took up a rust-red work cloth and cleaning solution bottle. Safety measures can't be over-stressed, we'd been told. "Always look out for things that might catch on moving parts," a supervisor once warned, "like clothing. One machine choked a fellow when ink rollers swallowed his necktie all the way up. Nasty." This day clothing didn't factor in. My carelessness brought pain, regardless.

I'll just wrap the rag around this forefinger, spray some solution, slide the cloth slowly—forward, backward along the roller. I hadn't factored the exposed gear cogs rotating steadily just beyond the ink rollers. Their teeth seized my cleaning rag. My fingertip followed, instantly yanked into the gear, bringing the equipment to a halt.

Now I lay on my back atop a First Aid surgical table. Someone positioned an extension to support my outstretched right arm. Catching the image of a nurse clicking a needle's syringe, I clenched my teeth. The three fingertip injections drew pain I've seldom known. Sweat beads sprung to my face in the cool room.

"This is to deaden the pain while we're treating your finger," a voice consoled. Really? During the nights passing I made a useful discovery. A pillow serves well for muzzling whimpers.

**

"So, Jerry. I hear you're looking to leave us?"

Machines had gone quiet in a rare printing lull. My colleague, Frankie, stepped across to my work area. Taking a cloth to his ink-spotted thumb, he spoke of the resignation notice I had given our company the day before. I nodded his way. "Yeah."

"We'll miss you around here."

Smiling, I acknowledged his thoughtfulness.

"Well, with you going off to San Antonio—Bible school is it?—I'm sure you've got a job waiting for you?"

"Actually, Frankie, no. I don't. Not yet."

"Really? No job? Wow." His forehead squeezed wrinkles into view as he moved toward his machine. Three minutes later he was back.

"Uh, Jerry." He resumed the visit as though no break occurred, his voice pensive. "No job yet? Uh, what will you do about food and stuff?"

For possibly the first time, my own thoughts drifted more seriously to the issue of provision, security.

"Well, things will come together." I felt my tone lacked the conviction I had intended.

"Mm, Jerry."

"Yeah?"

"How about the payments on your car? How do you plan to make those?" With my wife's work as a keypunch operator for an oil company, we had traded the Karmann Ghia clunker for a sleek Aleutian blue Pontiac Tempest.

"Well, I'm not really sure. But I believe God will provide."

In a tone only slightly less confident than my own, Frankie muttered, "Looks like he'll sure have to."

The exchange ended. So I thought. Frankie returned to his equipment. Then, moments later, came again to my post. His question, this time, was rhetorical.

"So, Jerry. Can I ask you this... What does your wife think of starving to death?"

I had recovered fairly quickly from my lapse in trust over my own future wellbeing. Frankie's words—sarcastic but lacking meanness—raised a grin to my lips. The wall clock indicated the shift winding down. Frankie, wagging his head slowly, lumbered over to his machine.

CHAPTER SEVENTEEN

SOUTHWARD

"Ah, I've been waiting for you!" Not surprised by the parcel's mute response, I noted the packet's address—International Bible College, San Antonio, Texas. A memory from long ago stirred.

The green 1950 Ford's exterior had been taking a steady rain drenching as my brother, Tim and I, settled into the back seat. I was still shivering when I smiled to the stooped figure who had just appeared beyond my window. The beam of his flashlight flickered back and forth on our eyes, to Tim's, then mine, then Tim's.

Old Pastor Schrader, his hat snugged down so the breeze couldn't lift it, chuckled loudly enough to overcome the sound of pounding rain. "Brother Lout", he called to my dad, "those are two very fine gentlemen you're hauling around back there." Dad nodded a thank you as he turned the ignition. The car's heater was yet to kick in but I sat there feeling warm on the inside. Dear old Brother Schrader—walking us out to the car in the rain, then standing there to give his goodbye—just for the kindness of it. *I hope I'm like that when I'm old.*

We had adopted Okmulgee's House of Prayer as our place of worship when we moved from California back to mom and dad's home state. After a time, good Pastor Schrader became ill. He passed away not long afterwards. A replacement pastor came and we changed to another church. One day a friend of my mother's called to her, "Thelma, you remember the Schrader's stately blond-haired daughter Hope? I understand she's gotten engaged. Marrying a young San Antonio fellow who grew up in Japan." The friend went on, "Hope's new husband teaches in a school his father founded near the end of the war, "International Bible College."

***

"Drive safe, Jerry." Smiling, my dad winked toward Ann, "That's our new daughter you've got with you there." He gave the Tempest a light tap and we turned from the gravel driveway onto Highway 75. The simple turning of the wheel, facing us southward, felt symbolic. Beyond the Oklahoma - Texas state line lay horizons, not one but many, I surmised. Landscapes of visions, dreams of service in some useful calling—a bigger task than we could ever bring about—bigger than who we were. We were moving further still from Ann's childhood home, yet we seemed carried forward to wide places ahead, like Montana's nickname suggests. Big Sky.

We passed the rolling, tree-marked cemetery beyond my own hometown. I glanced in the rear view mirror and picked up my earlier thought. *We've turned a corner.* I smiled at my young wife—lovely, courageous, Rocky Mountain lady.

What uncertainties lay ahead for her and me? If I could only know. A co-worker's question of a few days earlier had teased my resolve. . . "So what does your wife think of starving to death?"

I certainly felt my own misgivings at times. Weaknesses that weren't just physical dogged me. Whatever might lie ahead, I had little doubt that limping could well define some of the journey for me. I rolled my shoulders slowly about, willing myself from a melancholy drift.

My special passenger sat quietly. I tilted my head her way. "You still OK with this, darlin'?"

Ann nodded, smiling.

"Just a little scared, maybe?" I pressed. A second nod, but the smile remained.

Taking in a blue sky, I gave voice to what we both felt, "OK, Lord. We're yours."

The animal stockyards passed to our right a mile outside Okmulgee, providing a pungent aroma through the car's open windows. As a kid I accompanied my father to auctions held there — straw hat tipped forward like the grown-up rancher-men, a blade of long grass moving about like a probing antenna out my teeth. Seconds beyond the stockyards and continuing south, we crossed the Deep Fork River bridge. My spirit had rallied. From a suddenly happy place inside me, I almost shouted it: "Lone Star State—here we come!"

Memories of her Montana childhood surfaced in Ann's mind. She recalled a modest home, a living room scene one Sunday evening, a nine-year-old declaring for herself an overseas destiny.

Mystery – reserve – adventure – trust. All seemed to mingle. Her voice came steady and clear, carrying a resiliency I had only begun to discover.

"Yes. Texas. And after that, Africa."

www.kennymundsministry.org

Lyrics: Zacchaeus, This Little Light, Deep and Wide, I'll Go Where You Want me to Go. Public domain

Quote (p 25) often attributed to Will Rogers though unverified. Used by Permission
Will Rogers Memorial Museum

Made in the USA
Columbia, SC
10 June 2018